NIGEL HOLMES

PICT⊕RIAL
MAPS

THE HERBERT PRESS

Copyright © 1991 Nigel Holmes
Copyright under the Berne Convention

First published in the USA 1991

First published in Great Britain 1992 by
The Herbert Press Ltd, 46 Northchurch Road, London N1 1EJ

Printed and bound in Singapore

A CIP catalogue record for this book is available from the
British Library.

ISBN 1–871569–43–5

To Erin

Acknowledgments

I'd been *thinking* about this book for a long time, but it was actually *written* during 1990 and early 1991, when my wife was continuing her studies at Columbia University. My eternal thanks go to you, Erin. The hours that you had to put in studying Latin, Restoration Drama, The History of Western Political Thought, and other Heavy Stuff helped me to concentrate too. Thank you for getting me to write more clearly about things you read here and didn't understand. In every case, your thoughts made this book better. To have as a mate someone like you is a gift from heaven. Or somewhere.

Erin's attachment to Columbia meant also that I was introduced to the pleasures of going to the Rare Books and Manuscript Library there. The care with which the librarians bring you the hallowed volumes you've asked to see—a John Speed atlas from 1627, a Mercator atlas from 1635—is a wonderful thing. One's respect for the books grows even more when the librarian gives you one of those marvellously soft, velvet-covered, sausage-shaped bean bags to place on the pages to keep them open, eliminating the possibility that anything so toxic as your hands should do the job. Thanks for looking after the books so well, and allowing me the privilege of consulting them.

And thank you to these colleagues at *Time*: Rudy Hoglund, the art director of the magazine, my boss, and friend of fourteen years, for continued sympathetic understanding of the dual role I play there—that of full-time employee, and part-time distracted author; Paul Pugliese, our chief cartographer, who seems to be able to pull a map of anywhere in the world out of a drawer in some part of the office or his home, for a great deal of guidance about projections in general, for drawing the different examples of world projections in chapter 6, for correcting the text of that part of the book, and for keeping us groaning in the office with some of the worst jokes ever to come out of the mouth of a mapmaker; Rose Keyser, picture editor, for helping me to find exactly what I wanted to show here; Joe Lertola, senior chart designer, for taking so much of the burden of my real job off my shoulders in such an excellent way; and to the other members of the map and chart department, the researchers Noel McCoy and Deborah Wells, the artists Steve Hart and Nino Telak, for being as loyal and talented and funny a group of coworkers as anyone could wish for.

At Watson-Guptill, a big thank-you to Candace Raney for getting the book off the ground, to Carl Rosen for carefully restricting the sometimes overly informal nature of my writing, but always taking the time to explain why he advised against a particular turn of phrase, and to Bob Fillie, who now completes a trio of excellent designs for my Watson-Guptill books.

Finally, a word of thanks to the Macintosh, whose presence at *Time* has changed our lives in a pleasantly irreversible way. Many of the images here were drawn on the Mac, and all the words went through its miraculous guts at least three times. However did we do anything before?

Contents

1

Introduction

**An early crime
Life at home
Atlas maps and pictorial maps
Who needs this book?**

committed a crime when I was seven. An atlas made me do it. I stole it from my brother by simply erasing his name inside and putting mine in its place—an easy, if immoral, way to ensure that it was no longer his.

The stolen book was a children's pictorial atlas of the British Isles, crammed with wonderful little drawings of people standing on the maps. The people were farming, mining, traveling, banking, dancing; the energy and color of the crowded pictures made everyone practically jump off the pages. I loved this atlas, and long after I should have been consulting a more grownup one, I kept going back to it for reference. That book was important to me because it made geography interesting by combining pictures of things that I could relate to—buildings, trees, and people—with the usual abstract representations of the landmasses.

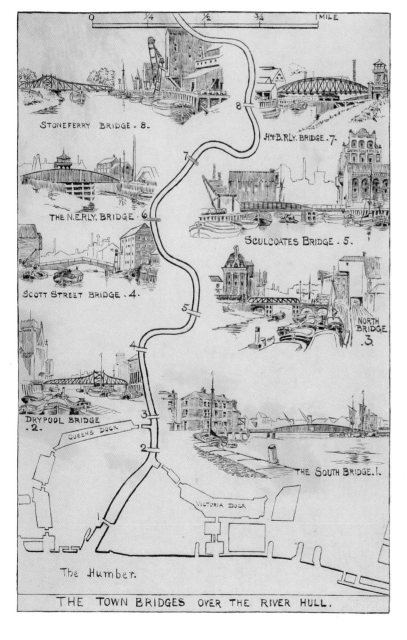

I really liked Uncle George's map of the bridges over the river Hull, in Yorkshire, drawn some time in the 1930s. It hung in the living room of my parents' house, which was about ten miles from the city of Hull. For the first time I realized that there was something more to maps than geography. The simple treatment of the river winding through the bridges is drawn with the same kind of relaxed lines as the pictures around it, but the lack of shading on the river separates it nicely from the buildings, clearly stating, ''this is the map *part, the other drawings are what the place* looks like.''

Here are pages from the Pictorial Atlas of the British Isles. *As a young child, I stared at the images in this book and longed to be able to draw that way. Later, at school, it was the perfect escape from academic geography lessons, and even though the maps were more artistic than factual, they gave a great overview of the diversity of Britain's terrain, the people who lived there, their industries and pastimes. The mining and mill towns of Sheffield, Bradford, and Halifax; Wensleydale cheesemaking; the Lake District; the Yorkshire Moors; bathing in the incredibly cold North Sea; Robin Hood and his Merry Men . . . it was all there.*

While England's hills roll gently and are drawn with soft green shadows, those in Wales are harsh and black, befitting the rugged countryside. The Welsh tradition of music and song is well represented by a band marching through the mountains; a lively sense of fun flows everywhere. The detailed and much more serious gazetteer at the back of the book explains the origins of place-names, giving young readers such diverse facts as when potatoes were introduced to England from America and the origin of the phrase "beyond the pale" (the Pale was the part of Ireland ruled by English law. If you didn't live within it, you were an outsider).

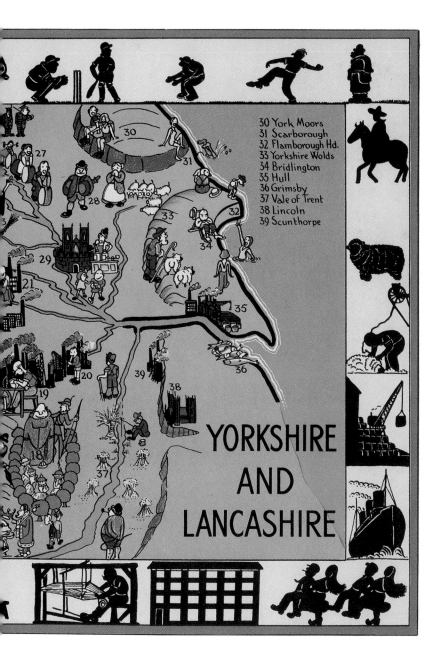

30 York Moors
31 Scarborough
32 Flamborough Hd.
33 Yorkshire Wolds
34 Bridlington
35 Hull
36 Grimsby
37 Vale of Trent
38 Lincoln
39 Scunthorpe

YORKSHIRE
AND
LANCASHIRE

NEIGHBOURS

This atlas was published in 1937, on the eve of World War II. The last map goes outside the British Isles, to neighbors in Europe and beyond. Germany and France eye each other from simplified fortifications. The gazetteer warns: "There are rumours of war, and war is foul wickedness. This devilish lunacy must not start. Ordinary humble folks in different countries do not want it." The happy little characters on the maps would soon be plunged into six years of conflict.

Apart from my brother's atlas, there was another "map" influence at home. My father's brother, George, was an artist who drew maps of Yorkshire, England. He drew one that showed all the bridges over the river Hull. I used to stare at the bridges, wondering how he had been able to draw them from a bird's-eye view. Like the maps in my brother's atlas, Uncle George's piece was a real map, but with pictures on it.

We also had a small map of Yorkshire by John Speed, one of the pioneer English mapmakers of the 1600s, that was covered with little three-dimensional hills and place-names that were quaintly different from their modern spellings. Our village was missing, and this was my first lesson in the passage of time—the place that I lived in hadn't been there forever.

How far can you see?	
Flying altitude (feet)	Distance to the horizon (miles)
5,000	86
10,000	122
15,000	149
20,000	173
25,000	193
30,000	211
35,000	228
40,000	244

Flying altitude: 3,500 feet (6.6 miles)

View from airplane window to the horizon: 228 miles

Ever wondered how far you can see from your window seat?

Symbols and drawings not only enliven a map, they tell you in detail what the map is about: not just weather—rain; not just war—tank positions.

Whether or not these three experiences had anything to do with it, I found as I grew up that whenever I traveled, I had to consult a map before leaving, during the trip, and upon arrival. Perhaps this is just the cartographic equivalent of leaving a trail of stones behind me, so that I can always retrace my steps. But for whatever deep psychological reason, I always have my head in a map, rather than taking in the view on even the simplest car journey. Sometimes the habit can pay unexpected dividends. It's quite a thrill to look out of an airplane window and recognize a shape on the ground from the map in your hands. If by chance you have actually *drawn* that coastline, or that mountain range 35,000 feet below you, the heart skips a beat as you confront the ultimate fact-check before your very eyes!

If you hadn't realized if before, the plane flight makes you understand what simplification is all about. How much should the mapmaker put in to convey a sense of a place? How much to leave out for the sake of clarity? When is a map better as a diagram than as a picture?

Comparing Atlas Maps and Pictorial Maps
This book is not about the sort of maps that one finds in a modern reference atlas. Users of an atlas bring their own agenda to the reading process. The atlas is read with a mission; something

needs to be found out from the basic factual well of information. Atlas maps are like the gameboard before the game has begun. All the pieces are in position, but no one is playing yet. A pictorial map, however, is a different game, one where the information from the atlas is rearranged in order to highlight some part of it. Perhaps you need to emphasize the bridges over a city river. You could remove the bridge symbols from the atlas map and replace them with realistic, out-of-scale bridge renderings, so that they now command attention as the focus of the rearranged map. Atlas maps are the starting points for all such pictorial versions: there has to be some base to work from, however unmap-like the final result may be. In the atlas itself, nothing distracts the eye too much, nor calls attention to any particular part of the map. After all, the cartographer does not know what detail you are looking for; maybe it wasn't the bridges. *Atlas* maps are pure reference. You go in there and choose what you want to see.

A *pictorial* map, however, always makes a point beyond the basic presentation of information. It concentrates the readers' attention on some part of itself, announcing its subject clearly—and pictorially. It is therefore different from the atlas map in that it has a specific message. For example, it might tell you that today's *weather* will be cloudy; or the *tanks* moved in this direction; or the *bridges* are here (using three-dimensional representations of what they look like).

Some of the maps in this book fall outside this definition. In some cases they might simply be the geographic shape of the United States, filled in with cars or logs or whatever, showing an advertiser's national sales network, or that the advertiser is proud to be American and wants to share it with us.

From a 1985 New York and New Jersey Port Authority advertisement, these controlled and detailed drawings of the major bridges around Manhattan work very well in their small space. Among a host of facts, the accompanying text tells the reader that the George Washington Bridge (1 on the map), carries more traffic daily than any other bridge in the world, and that the public liked the look of the original bare steel so much that plans to clad it in granite were never completed.

Flag-waving at its most extreme. The shape of America combined with the stars and stripes emphasizes the ''proud to be American'' message in many advertising logos and images.

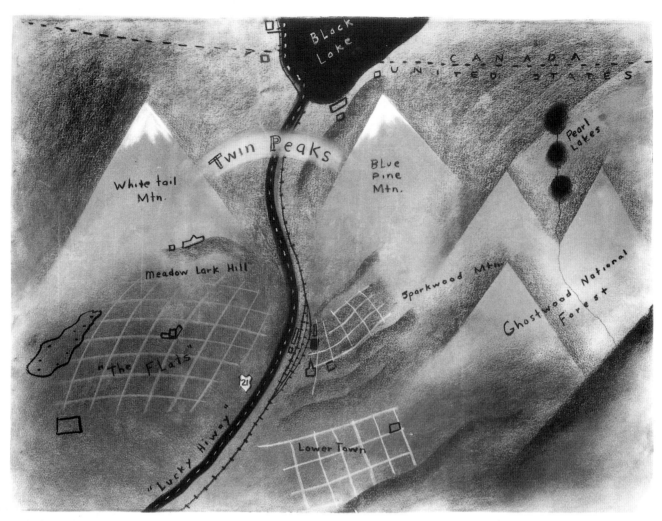

The map shows: Black Lake, CANADA, UNITED STATES, Pearl Lakes, Twin Peaks, White tail Mtn., Blue Pine Mtn., Meadow Lark Hill, Sparkwood Mtn., Ghostwood National Forest, "the Flats", 21, "Lucky Hiwey", Lower Town

David Lynch's map of the town of Twin Peaks was used by Lynch and producer Mark Frost to help explain their series idea to executives at ABC television, even before turning in a pilot script.

A Sense of Place

Before showing the pilot script of his revolutionary show *Twin Peaks* to executives at ABC television, director David Lynch drew a map to give them an idea of where the action would unfold. The peaks of the title, and the town they name, are clearly visible as white-topped mountains rising out of the modeled landscape. By creating a sense of place, Lynch made the town all the more believable. A straightforward map would have been dull by comparison and might have suggested that there was something intrinsically interesting about the *geography* of the place. What was much more important to convey was the mood of the story, and it's nicely captured in Lynch's quirky drawing. Not many maps in this book attempt to convey both a mood and data, but it can be done, and Lynch's map shows that information can be imbued with emotion and retain its factual authority.

One of the best-selling posters at the Museum of Modern Art in New York is Jasper Johns's *Map*, painted in 1961. The original hangs in the museum entrance. Apart from its qualities as a work of art, it is a wonderful celebration of America. It is a recognizable symbol of a place we know, glorified by being painted so large (six-by-ten feet) and elevated to a position of importance in a major museum. America deserves that sort of pedestal. As mapmakers we can forgive Johns's use of the same bright blue for some of the states and the surrounding oceans, because he's an artist and not a cartographer.

Who This Book Is For

I hope this collection of ideas about maps excites you in the way that Jasper Johns's painting excites thousands of museum-goers. If you make maps professionally, or commission them for newspapers, magazines, books, or exhibitions, there are suggestions and ideas contained in the examples shown that lead you away from the run-of-the-mill *locators* that your clients or editors might expect of you. The advent of the computer has meant that more and more people are able to produce maps, especially with the help of specific cartographic drawing programs. These technical wonders equip aspiring artists with map bases in a variety of different projections (for more about the computer, and about projections, see chap. 6 below). As with all new technology, the excellence of such maps does not depend so much on the program used as on the person using it.

This book might also do a little to foster or rekindle an interest in geography. It is alarming how poorly we remember what's what in the world of place-names (if we ever knew them in the

Jasper Johns's Map *(1961) hangs in the entrance to New York's Museum of Modern Art, colorfully celebrating both America and the art of maps.*

15

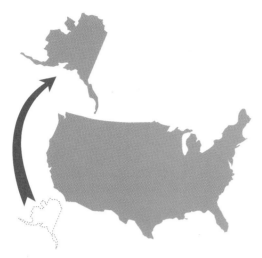

For graphic economy, most maps tuck Alaska into the space below California. In January 1990, to counter this misrepresentation, and the resulting confusion in students' minds about where the state really is, the Alaska state legislature passed a resolution "respectfully requesting that all major United States magazines, newspapers, textbook publishers, and map publishers . . . place Alaska in its correct geographical position . . . in the northwest corner." Watch for the let's-make-Alaska-proportionately-the-right-size campaign next. It's one-fifth of the size of the United States, but is usually shown much smaller.

first place). A friend who lectures on newspaper design and editing is fond of embarrassing well-informed audiences by giving them a map of the world printed with country borders but no names. Very few people can complete a request to fill in the locations of, say, El Salvador, Belize, Ecuador, Madagascar, Benin, Gabon, and Bhutan. "Too obscure," they object. Then how about Algeria, Tunisia, Libya, Egypt, Sudan, Ethiopia, and Somalia? (Once you know, it's easy—they run in the above order along the north rim of Africa and down the Red Sea).

In January 1990, I received a letter from the office of the governor of Alaska, asking that we position that state in its proper geographic place on maps of the United States appearing in *Time* magazine. Too many schoolchildren thought that Alaska was an island south of California. They had seen it that way on most maps. We agreed to join in their effort to correct this mistake.

To those information-graphics artists who have asked me where they can get help with their maps, or simply how they can make their maps more interesting, I hope that this book will be a starting gate from which to launch lively, sometimes amusing, and occasionally provocative but always *informative* views of the world.

And to those who have no intention of ever making a map themselves, here are some of the most beautiful examples ever drawn, for your viewing enjoyment. Gaze at them and dream of exotic places to be explored someday. But when you just want to

As geographers and explorers pieced together facts about the earth's surface, the clouds were rolled back on the emerging picture. This page from an 1835 school atlas shows that progress.

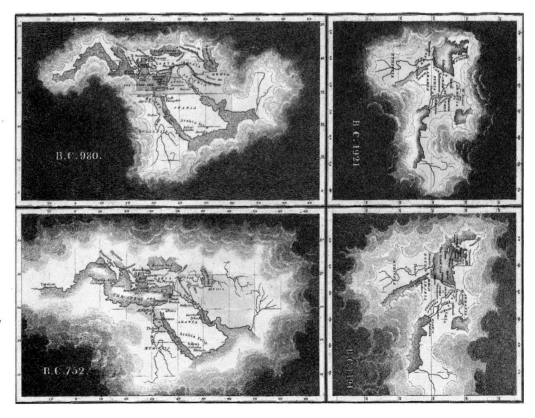

invite a friend or two over to your house next week, and they dont't know where you live, consult the section on making maps for your friends (see chap. 7).

What is it about maps that intrigues us? Why do we pore over them endlessly? The answer can be found in an earlier era, before much of the earth was explored. Maps lessened the fear of the unknown and looked authoritative, even though there were blank spaces filled with animals, compasses, or cartouches, and some of the supposedly known areas were incorrectly drawn. Maps, however, opened up the imagination to faraway places while comfortably confirming what was known of the immediate surroundings. By making a diagram of something, you are confronting it, even if you don't fully understand it.

The road map in the glove compartment is the adult's security blanket. We won't get lost, we've got the map. We forgive its inaccuracies, and we accept the mapmaker's conventions, which Huckleberry Finn could not when he and Tom Sawyer were blown east in a balloon. Huck insisted that they were not over Indiana yet because the color of the land hadn't changed to pink from the green of Illinois that he knew from his school atlas.

James Gillray's (1757–1815) drawing of Napoleon and Pitt carving up the world has entered the graphic design compendium of chiché, but no subsequent rip-off of this image has approached the juiciness of the original. What this drawing did was to make the globe into a symbol that could be pushed and pulled and massaged or cut into any shape by cartoonists of the future, and it opened up possibilities with maps that political cartoonists are still exploiting today. Gillray's caption for his cartoon was, "The plumb pudding in danger, or State epicures taking un petit souper."

2

History

**The "first" map
From Ptolemy through the Middle Ages to Mercator
A Californian artist**

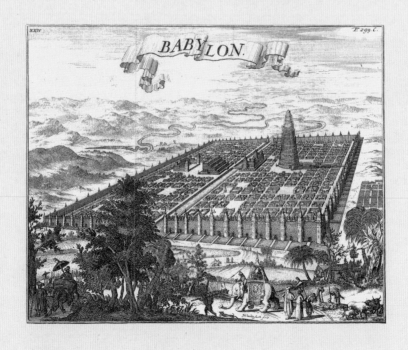

he first map? It was a simple gesture:  [The cave is *that* way]. More of a performance, really; a map drawn in the air. The gestures that we use today, to bridge the language gap when we shop in Rome or ask directions in Athens, are probably the same ones used by our skin-clad ancestors in paleolithic times. No gesturer, of course, survives from a century ago, let alone five hundred. So what's the first surviving *graphic* map? According to most historians, the leading contender for the ''world's oldest'' is the map of a river-valley engraved on a hand-sized clay tablet found near Babylon and dated 2300 B.C.

Ancient Babylon, about fifty-five miles south of present-day Baghdad, had a couple of really bad mishaps after this map was made. First the city was destroyed by the Assyrians in 689 B.C. (our clay tablet was already sixteen hundred years old by then). Then Babylon made a comeback, and even successfully bid to be the site of the forerunner of the Strip at Las Vegas—the Hanging Gardens—but it was completely abandoned in 275 B.C. when the Seleucid dynasty built themselves a new capital, so disgusted were they at the immoral goings-on around the Sixth Wonder of the World. Yet through it all, the diagrammatic record of land ownership, scratched onto a little piece of clay, survived. If that was one fantastic physical feat of endurance, the Babylonians

This is the oldest-known map: an inscribed, baked clay tablet (3 × 2½ in.) from 2300 B.C., found at the site of ancient Gazur (now Yorghan Tepe, Iraq) in 1930–31. The map is a record of land ownership—recorded not so much for pure geography, as for the government to be able to levy taxes—oriented with west at the bottom. The plot of land marked in the center is three acres. Lines running past it probably represent the Euphrates River. Beyond that, on both sides, are mountain ranges rendered in a fish-scale pattern.

The earliest maps have been found in the ground some miles to the north of Nebuchadnezzar's infamous city of Babylon, shown at left in an engraving from 1708. King Nebuchadnezzar II (605–561 B.C.) spent most of his 43-year reign rebuilding the ancient city. The outer enclosure was about the size of New York City. In the middle distance is the Ziggurat, known to the Hebrews as the Tower of Babel. It was actually built as an observatory to study stars. Most fascinating of all the city's splendors was the 32-acre Hanging Gardens built on the east bank of the Euphrates by Nebuchadnezzar to placate the homesickness of his Persian concubine.

19

This painted pottery fragment (ca. 3800 B.C.) was found at Tepe Gawra in northern Iraq. Do these marks represent actual *mountain ranges with a river flowing between them, or were mountains and rivers merely the inspiration for a nice* decoration*? If they represent actual geography, then this is a map (and it would be 1,500 years older than the so-called oldest map).*

A perspective on time: The lengths of geological ages become understandable when you can see them in scale. Note that cartographers of today are closer in time to Mercator than he was to Ptolemy. It's all too easy to think of history as a single way-back-then lump.

scored an equally long-lasting point for cartography with their mathematical numerical system, which led to the division of the circle into 360 degrees.

But the "world's oldest" map may have a rival, in fact, many rivals. New research is pushing the age of cartography much further back in time. It is now thought that prehistoric cave paintings contained maps of a kind. While most historians have concentrated on the parts of prehistoric art that are recognizable—animals and human figures—those elements are far outnumbered by abstract geometric signs. These squares, circles, and other shapes are sometimes connected by lines: Could they be maps? Paleolithic (60,000 to 30,000 B.C.) landscapes do occasionally include buildings in plan form, but I am not convinced that their creators were consciously making maps. Similar claims (although for a much younger map) are made for a pottery jar found at Tepe Gawra in 1950, which dates from around 3800 B.C.

For me, the painting on the Tepe Gawra jar is *decoration*. When the artist drew these two rows of triangles with a hairy, snaking line between them, was he or she really drawing mountains and a river? I'll admit that there are less ambiguous examples of prehistoric maps, in which there are images that actually look like settlement plans, are less decorative, and therefore were possibly drawn as *information*. Certainly one could argue that primitive people had reason to record the positions of dwellings. But when it comes to landscapes, and the chance to paint one on pottery, it seems that the artist might have painted inverted triangles with only the slightest, if any, intention of making them represent *mountains*, let alone a specific place. Only if the artist had meant to represent such a specific place could the result be called a map.

I imagined that what I would see when confronted with early maps would be naive drawings with primitive cyphers for trees and mountains and mammoths for decoration. On the contrary, by the time one stops bickering about whether the thing is actually a map or not, many maps from roughly 4,500 years ago

Cave paintings
and other rock art
in France and Spain

| 30,000 bc | 25,000 bc | 20,000 bc | 15,000 bc |

Upper Paleolithic Period

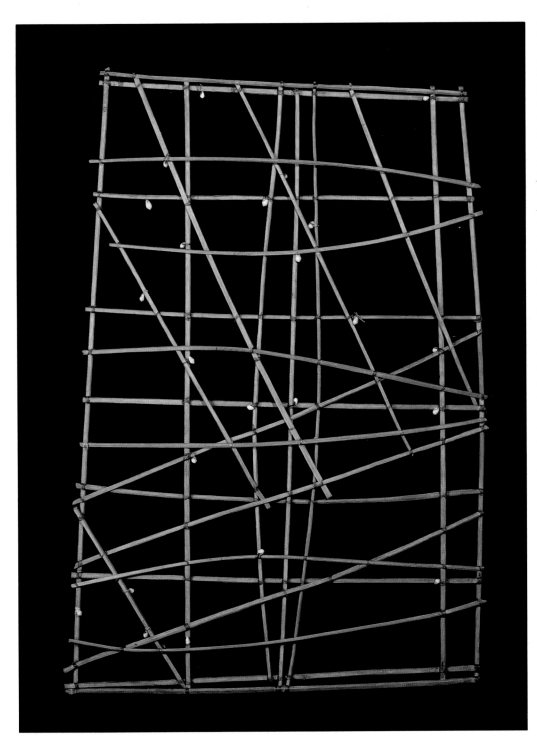

This nineteenth-century palmstick sea-chart shows a roughly 500-mile area around the Marshall Islands in the Pacific. The outer frame represents the sea, interior curved twigs the prevailing wave-fronts. The shells, attached with coconut fibers, stand for islands, and threads let canoe navigators know when they could expect to see the islands appear on the horizon. These portable diagrams were used until the middle of the nineteenth century. Although grid-lines had been invented 2,000 years earlier, there was a structural necessity for them here, and these extra "lines" on the map must have helped the islanders keep on course more easily.

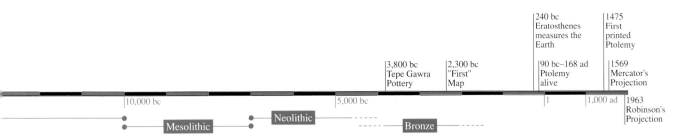

| | | 240 bc
Eratosthenes
measures the
Earth | 1475
First
printed
Ptolemy |
| | 3,800 bc
Tepe Gawra
Pottery | 2,300 bc
"First"
Map | 90 bc–168 ad
Ptolemy
alive | 1569
Mercator's
Projection |

10,000 bc   5,000 bc   1   1,000 ad   1963
Robinson's
Projection

Mesolithic   Neolithic   Bronze

Eskimo driftwood carvings of coastlines had to be accurate because Eskimo industry depended on an intimate knowledge of inlets and rivers—for example, fishermen needed to know how many bays from home they were.

are very precise pieces of straightforward cartography, and the reason that they were so geographically correct was that they covered only small areas. The immediate neighborhood was known and drawn, but what lay beyond was definitely a mystery. Imagine a world with no satellites, airplanes, ships, cameras, or *maps*. Trying to figure out your surroundings would be like an ant trying to do the same for a patch of kitchen floor. The ant would hardly comprehend the pattern on one floor tile, let alone how that pattern repeats, then meets a different kind of terrain (for example, carpet), and so on, throughout the rest of the house. If you think of the ant on the floor, humans are a million times *smaller* in relation to the earth. It's not surprising that early attempts to plot the shape of the world were full of false starts and wild guesses. And in *terra incognita*, the scientific cartographer became the imaginative artist: Pictures of exotic animals, ornate compass-roses, or cherubs blowing in the direction of the prevailing winds would fill up the blanks.

Back at the local level there was no need to fill up blank spaces on the map. Eskimos, for example, plotted the shorelines around Hudson Bay's Belcher Islands with an accuracy that went unrivaled until modern times. Their livelihood depended on an intimate knowledge of inlets and rivers, so they had to get it right. Likewise, the Marshall Islanders made incredible bamboo diagrams of the sea surrounding their Pacific home. It's amazing to think that these maps were produced by people who had not yet invented a written language for themselves. In the 1830s, the British naval officer Sir James Ross found that Eskimos not only understood his charts, but were able to extend the shorelines far beyond what he and other explorers knew.

Elephants and Galleons

Among really early mapmakers, the Aztecs were one people who did decorate their work. They regarded maps in a different light from the Eskimos or Marshall Islanders. Rather than making a road map, which would help you find your way (or your fish), their maps recorded events and history. Trees, rivers, and buildings were drawn naturalistically. The names of towns were represented by drawings of people. As such, Aztec maps are the real forerunners of many of the pictorial maps in this book.

This verse by Jonathan Swift* is often quoted in books about old maps:

> So Geographers in *Afric*-Maps
> With savage Pictures fill their gaps
> And o'er uninhabitable Downs
> Place Elephants for want of Towns.

*From *On Poetry: A Rhapsody* (1667–1745).

Most commentators use this to introduce the thesis that illustrations on maps are space fillers disguising a lack of information. Later, the theory goes, there would be no need to fill up anything—there would be *geography* to put in there. Only Wilma George in her excellent book *Animals and Maps* suggests otherwise: "The possibility that elephants did, indeed, occupy land where there were no towns seems to have been overlooked. It seems never to have been accepted that the animals on many a famous map were neither fictitious in their form nor haphazardly placed around the world."

A good point. Why *not* put indigenous animals or vegetation, or even prominent landmarks in an otherwise unmarked—as opposed to uncharted—area of a map? And why not put ships in the sea, sailing in the direction of the prevailing winds?

What galleons and elephants teach us is that *decoration* need not be a dirty word. Often referred to as "mere" decoration, informative pictorial additions to maps can both delight and instruct (and fill up those pesky blank spaces).

The Earth as a Sphere

The father of Greek literature, Homer, considered the earth to be a flat disk surrounded by water. The sun rose from the ocean in

This detail above from a migration scroll (ca. 1400) shows the Aztecs leaving their homeland (Azatlan). Apart from the presence of the man in a boat, no graphic attempt is made to distinguish water from land. But the footprints help!

Using illustrations to fill up blank spaces on maps might at first have been a substitute for lack of geographical knowledge, but elephants and galleons don't have to be merely decorative elements: there are elephants in Africa, and galleons indicate wind and current direction.

the morning and sank back into it at the end of the day. However great Homer was, his fellow Greeks pretty soon began to question his theory (later scholars even questioned his very existence). Their argument was simple: Observation led them to understand what was actually happening around them, and in the sixth century B.C. Aristotle concluded that ''the sphericity of the Earth is proved by the evidence of our senses.'' He noticed not only the movement of the stars in the sky, but also, as he traveled, brand new stars appearing on the horizon. Furthermore, when ships came into view, he could see the sails first, then the hull. If the earth was flat, the whole ship would appear as a tiny dot and gradually get bigger. Something else: the Greeks saw that the shadow that earth cast on the moon was not a straight line, it was curved. Once they knew that the earth was a sphere, the next question was, how big?

Four centuries passed before anyone came up with an accurate answer. Eratosthenes, who was in charge of the library at the great museum of Alexandria—it was called the *library*, but was actually more like a present-day think-tank—calculated the

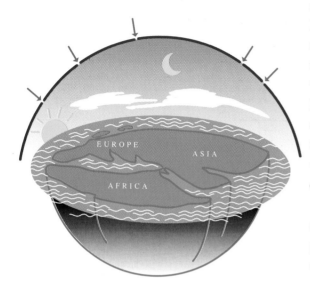

Homer thought of the world (above) as a hollow disk floating in a huge sea (Anaximander, before him, had considered it to be drum-shaped). Above this disk, or drum, was the firmament, with holes punched in it to let starlight shine through at night.

Most of what we know about Anaximander and other Greek cartographers comes from the writings of Strabo, whose own view of the world (right), was later taken as a starting point by Ptolemy.

Eratosthenes (276–196 B.C.) was the first person to measure the earth's size accurately (below), but his knowledge of the shapes of the continents on it was poor—he, of course, was limited by what was known at the time. Although his map is lost, enough descriptions of it survive to enable modern reconstructions (right). The southern part of Eratosthenes' map is shortened because it was believed that the seas near the equator were too hot for navigation.

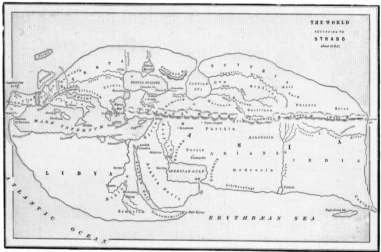

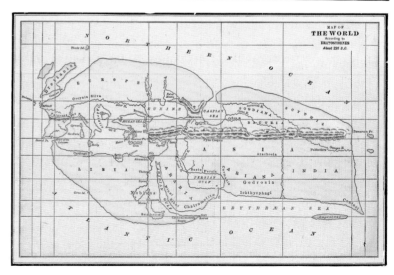

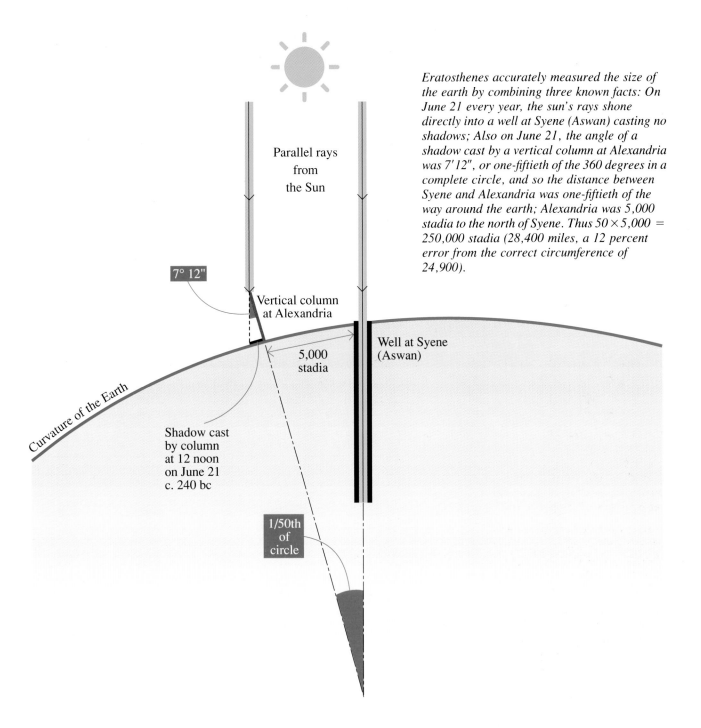

Parallel rays
from
the Sun

7° 12"

Vertical column
at Alexandria

5,000
stadia

Well at Syene
(Aswan)

Curvature of the Earth

Shadow cast
by column
at 12 noon
on June 21
c. 240 bc

1/50th
of
circle

Eratosthenes accurately measured the size of the earth by combining three known facts: On June 21 every year, the sun's rays shone directly into a well at Syene (Aswan) casting no shadows; Also on June 21, the angle of a shadow cast by a vertical column at Alexandria was 7'12", or one-fiftieth of the 360 degrees in a complete circle, and so the distance between Syene and Alexandria was one-fiftieth of the way around the earth; Alexandria was 5,000 stadia to the north of Syene. Thus 50 × 5,000 = 250,000 stadia (28,400 miles, a 12 percent error from the correct circumference of 24,900).

earth's circumference to be 28,400 miles. At that time, the unit of measurement was the *stadium*, which was roughly equivalent to 200 yards.* Eratosthenes knew that every year on June 21 the sun shone directly into a deep well at Syene (modern Aswan), illuminating the water at the bottom and thus marking a day when the sun was directly overhead there. His library was 5,000 stadia directly to the north of Syene. One year (around 240 B.C.), on June 21, he took note of the length of the shadow cast by a vertical column at Alexandria. Using simple geometry, he

*There is disagreement about the length of a stadium. Some sources put it at one tenth of a mile, or 176 yards. The Olympic Stadium was 630.8 feet, but one at Athens was 607 feet.

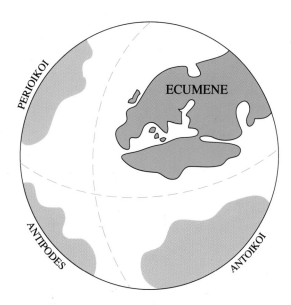

In 150 B.C. Crates plotted contemporary geography onto an Eratosthenes-sized earth and found that the landmasses covered only a quarter of it. Upset by such asymmetry, Crates created three imaginary continents to balance the known one. In so doing, he anticipated the Americas, Australia, and Antarctica.

calculated the angle of the shadow to be 7 degrees 12 minutes, which is about one fiftieth of the complete circle of 360 degrees. He thus knew that the distance between Alexandria, where he had measured the shadow, and Syene, where there was no shadow that day, was one fiftieth of the way round the Earth. Fifty times 5,000 equals 250,000 stadia, or 28,400 miles. He was only 12 percent off; we now know the Earth to be 24,900 miles round the equator.

Although Eratosthenes had fairly accurately measured the size of the sphere, he died not knowing much about the shapes of the landmasses on it.

As soon as artists and mapmakers understood that they lived on a big ball, they were faced with the problem of how to represent in two dimensions the shapes of the known continents. It was obvious to the Greeks that using a globe was the only way to show the continents in their proper proportions and in a true relationship to each other. In 100 B.C. Crates plotted the known world onto a globe. He drew the land in a scale that corresponded to Eratosthenes' estimate of the size of the sphere and found that it covered barely a quarter of the surface. This upset his idea of symmetry, so he added three imaginary continents, one to the south and two around the back. Crates' desire for everything to be neat and balanced thus gave us a first "view" of Australia and the Americas. Following his example, future mapmakers included a huge *Terra Australis* (Southern Continent) on their maps until 1773, when Captain James Cook went to have a good look at what was really there.

Ptolemy

The first attempt at a flat map of the whole world was made by Marinus of Tyre, who lived from A.D. 70 to 130. His seamans' charts were studied, and corrected, in *A Guide to the Delineation of the World*, completed in 160 by Ptolemy (Claudius Ptolemaeus), the man whose theory and practice would remain the cartographic standard for the next thousand years. His maps—faults and all—were copied, practically unchanged, until the late Middle Ages.

Cartographic artists have always had to start with some reference. In fact the more artistic we are, the more we have blindly relied on existing published shorelines. And we have to trust them; after all, there is no way to test their accuracy. Perhaps these days we'll use a computer atlas program to generate the shapes we need, but at the least we'll look them up in a printed atlas, the *Times*, or the *National Geographic*, and trace them as a starting point. So in the Middle Ages, Ptolemy's work was rediscovered, revered, and copied.

Ptolemy formulated the basic rules of mapmaking. He was a man of many interests, and he wrote two key books of the utmost importance to the blossoming field of cartography, the first on astronomy (*Almagest*), and the second on geography (*Geographia*). It is easy to point to Ptolemy's errors, and each of these books had a very basic error. In the *Almagest* he rejected the idea that the earth revolves around the sun, reverting instead to the idea that the Earth was the center of the universe. Even today we unwittingly cling to this notion in our references to the sun rising and setting. Only the soap opera has it right: *As the World Turns*. Then in *Geographia*, which included his rendition of the world (and twenty-six other regional maps) Ptolemy ignored Eratosthenes' estimate of the size of the earth, and relied instead on that of Strabo, a first century geographer who had mistakenly recorded the earth's circumference to be 180,000 stadia, instead of 250,000. Ptolemy's earth was thus three quarters of the real size.

But whatever his mistakes, Ptolemy's definition of geography went further than anyone before him, and for a long time to come afterward. He put forward the notion that maps should not only show obvious features like cities, rivers, and mountains, but could also include climate, population density, birth rates and incidences of disease. In other words, he saw maps as vehicles for information outside a literal depiction of what was on the ground. In the first words of the first chapter of his *Geographia* Ptolemy gave us all permission to draw on our maps, to add information, charts, and statistics: "Geography is a representation in picture of the whole known world together with the phenomena which are contained therein." He is careful, however, to make a distinction between *chorography* and *geography*. Chorography's concern is to "paint a true likeness, and not merely to give exact position and size. Geography, however, looks at the position and not the size." "Chorography needs an artist, and no one presents it rightly unless he is an artist." Ptolemy seems determined that his readers shall understand the difference: one branch of the science (chorography) being reserved for the graphic *description* of places, the other (geography) for its *position* on a map.

Ptolemy was concerned because his forerunners had been lazy about using scale properly. They were more interested in cramming everything into their maps than with being geographically accurate. If much was known about one area— say, Europe—and there were many names to write on the map, then that area would simply be enlarged to accommodate them. If little was known, a whole continent would be reduced, as with Africa. Ptolemy's answer to this graphic overcrowding problem

Ptolemy's influence on mapmaking was the greatest of any single person. Though they contained errors, the eight volumes of Ptolemy's great book Geographia *laid down the basic rules of mapmaking. It contained 28 maps and recorded 8,000 place-names, along with their latitudes and longitudes. Although it was written around A.D. 150,* Geographia *was unavailable to non-Greek readers until 1406, when Jacob Angelicus, in Florence, translated it. This engraving from an old atlas was shown at the annual general meeting of the American Geographical Society on February 11, 1879, in New York. The society's president, Charles Daly, delivered an address in which he emphatically confirmed Ptolemy's stature.*

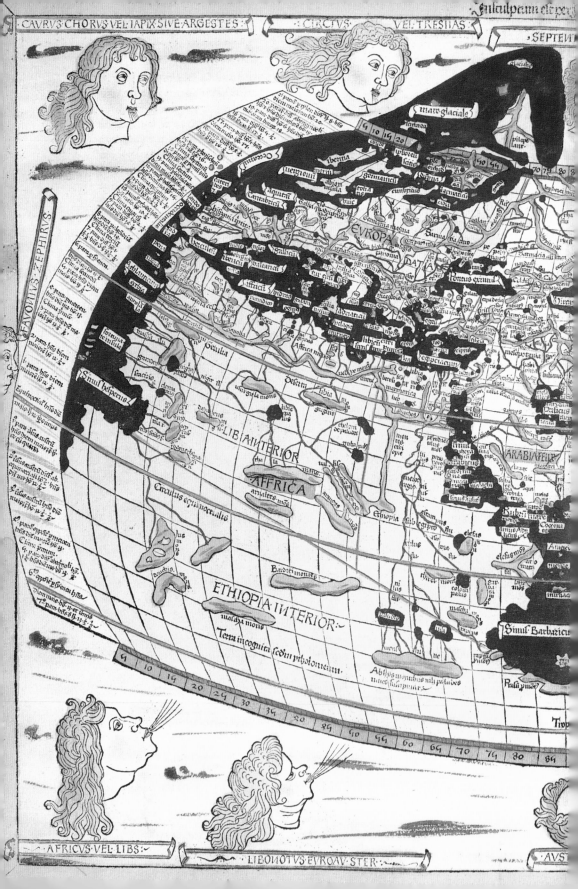

(Previous page) There are many versions of Ptolemy's maps. This one is from a 1482 edition of his Geographia, *and it shows the mistake he made concerning the Indian Ocean, which he drew as an enclosed, inland sea. Ptolemy included a large, imaginary river system in the western Sahara, and since he was unsure of the origin of the Nile, he created the "Mountains of the Moon" as its source. The discovery of this imaginary place became a prime goal for explorers until just over a hundred years ago. Using Strabo's calculations of the size of the earth (rather than the more accurate ones of Eratosthenes), Ptolemy drew a world that was about three-quarters of the real size. This would later lead Columbus to think he'd reached Asia when he landed in the Bahamas. This print shows degrees of latitude and longitude, and also a system of parallels (climata) that show the length of the longest day, from 12 hours at the equator to 24 on the Arctic Circle.*

in Europe was to include in his atlas close-up maps for the better-known areas. A larger scale could show more detail where it was needed: "In each map the same proportion must be kept throughout, as for example, when we describe the head alone we speak in terms of the head, or when we speak of the hand alone we speak in terms of the hand, and we do not figure equally for the head and the hand unless we are drawing a figure of the whole man in one image. And so it does not matter if we sometimes increase the size of the whole or sometimes lessen it . . . for instance, if there should be numerous localities in certain parts."

The old problem of how to represent a rounded surface on a flat one was an interesting challenge for him. He knew, like all his predecessors, that the only way to show the true relationships of landmasses was on a globe. But globes were hardly portable and would have to be really huge to show any detail. So he created the grid of longitude (length) and latitude (breadth) lines. Onto this grid of parallels and meridians he plotted what was known of the world, which he believed occupied half the circuit of the globe. He thus numbered his meridians 0–180 degrees from west to east, starting just west of Africa at the so-called Fortunate Isles (the Canary Islands) and ending near the present coast of Indochina. Latitudinally (from top to bottom), he numbered his parallels from 63 degrees north at the island of Thule to 16 degrees 25 minutes south in central Africa (*Terra Incognita*). Elsewhere in *Geographia*, Ptolemy discusses two other projections for representing the half-sphere he needed to show (*half*-sphere because he thought only half was occupied). He calculated the size of the known world to measure 4,734 miles from north to south, and 10,342 miles from east to west, and was the first to start drawing maps with north consistently at the top, reasoning that since most of the known world was in the north it would be easier to read if it was in the top half of a map.

In the introduction to the only English translation of Ptolemy's *Geographia*, by Edward Stevenson (1932), Joseph Fischer, a Ptolemy scholar, says, "If we wish today in retrospect to establish the history of a country or the destinies of a people of the ancient world, we shall always turn with very great profit to the maps and the text of Ptolemy. The location of places, the designation of the mountains and the rivers, the disposition of the tribes may propound to us many geographical and cartographical riddles, but there will be no lack of stimulus, and many a fortunate discovery will always reward serious occupation with the text and especially, with the maps of Ptolemy."

Two hundred and fifty years after Ptolemy died, the library in Alexandria where he had worked was destroyed. For a long while thereafter, cartography itself seemed to have died.

The following labels appear on the map:

Cathay · INDIA superior · Quinsai · FRANCISCA · C. Britonum · NO VVS · Exteriores · Hispania · Terra florida · Oceanus occidentalis · Medera · Archipelagus 7448 insularū · Chamaho · Panuco · Inf. Tortucarū · Fortunarę inf. · Zipangri · Temistitan · CVBA · Inf. Hesperidum · AFRICAE pars · Iucatana · Hispaniola · Seiana · Antilia · Iamica · Dominica · S. Iacobi · inf. fdonum · Beragna · PARIAS abundat auro & margaritis · Sinus Atlanticus · ORBIS · Canibali · Catigara · Insula Atlantica quam vocant Brasilij & Americam · Inf. infortunatę · Regio Gigantum · Calensuan · 7 insule Mar guentarū · Mare pacificum · Fretum Magalimu

Later editions of Ptolemy's Geographia *included up-to-date information and discoveries from explorers and geographers. This woodcut of the New World is from Münster's edition, printed in Basel about 1540. It names the Straits of Magellan.*

Three World Views

In the late Middle Ages there were three different ways for people to look at the physical world. First, there was rediscovered *Ptolemaic* geography; second, there was the study of *portolan* or navigational sea charts used by sailors and explorers; and third, there was the point of view of the *church*. The origins of these three types of map were reflected by their different audiences.

1. Ptolemaic Geography   One reason that the Middle Ages have been referred to as the Dark Ages is because most Western European scholars of the time didn't know Greek. This eliminated study of the best classical work during most of the Middle Ages. So for a thousand years after the death of Ptolemy, mapmaking stood still. Arabic translations of his writings and copies of his maps had survived, and they resurfaced in Europe in the thirteenth century. In 1406 Jacob Angelus translated *Geographia* into Latin. Manuscript copies were made, and the maps were redrawn. But it was the invention of printing that most furthered Ptolemy's posthumous fame. His first appearance in print was in 1475. The reproduction was by woodcuts, but very shortly afterward copperplate engraving was used. This was a

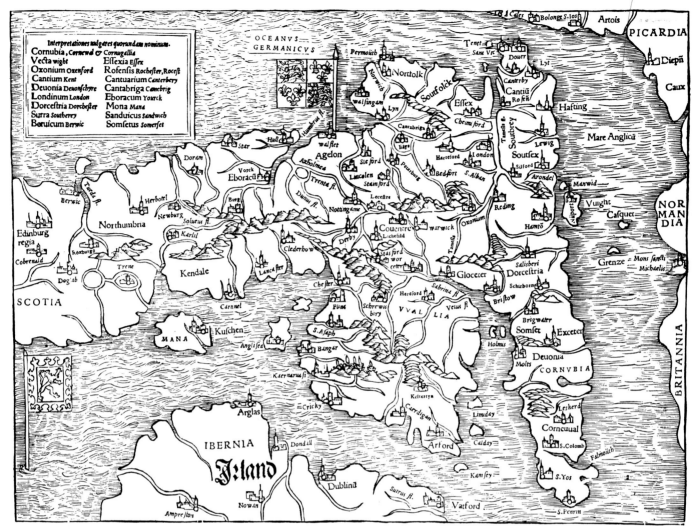

This woodcut from the 1540 edition of Geographia *is the first printed map of Britain. Each town is located by its own little pile of buildings. By turning the map on its side, with north at the left, the artist was able to make the image bigger in the space available. The national flags of England and Scotland are included.*

finer method of reproduction, allowing artists and printers greater control and precision of line.

Gradually the errors in Ptolemy's maps were reduced. First, Gerhardus Mercator, then Johannes Kepler, and finally Guillaume de l'Isle in 1700 corrected the size of the Mediterranean Sea, which had been a third too long. Sometimes errors have happy endings. Based on a Ptolemy-sized Earth, Columbus set off west imagining that if he sailed for 5,000 miles he would reach Asia. When he did hit land, he indeed thought that he had reached his goal. The distance from Spain to Asia, however, is actually 14,000 miles; Columbus hadn't even got to America proper; what he discovered in 1492 was the Bahamas. It was lucky for him too, since he didn't have enough food on board to last much longer. All that remains of his trip to Asia is that native Americans are called Indians.

Not only was America discovered by mistake, it got the wrong name, too. Martin Waldseemüller's world map of 1507 combined the handed-down knowledge of Ptolemy with the new discoveries of Columbus. Waldseemüller called the southern continent of the New World America, after he had read Amerigo Vespucci's extravagantly self-promoting claims on his return from a 1494 trip to Venezuela. Realizing the error, Waldseemüller left the name off subsequent maps, but to no avail: It stuck, as we know.

The voyage that really cleared up a lot of misconceptions about what was on the earth was led by Ferdinand Magellan in 1519. Five ships and two hundred men set out from Spain to the tip of South America, through the straits that now bear Magellan's name, and into an ocean that was so calm after rounding the Horn that Magellan called it Pacific (''peaceful''). Three years after starting, one ship returned to Spain. All but eighteen men had died. Magellan was not among the survivors, but his legacy was more important for geography than that of any of the early daredevil explorers.

2. Portolan Charts

The second type of map in use in the Middle Ages was the portolan, or harbor-finding chart. Essential for sailors, it was primarily concerned with the sea and its coastlines and little else. Such charts are characterized by a mass

This is a portolan chart showing the coast of North America from the Vallard Atlas *of 1547. It's a beautiful demonstration of picture and information in one map. The typical arrangement of lines and compasses is clearly evident here. There were strict conventions used in the preparation of these navigational charts: The principal wind directions were always drawn in black or gold, the ''half-winds'' were green, and the ''quarters,'' red.*

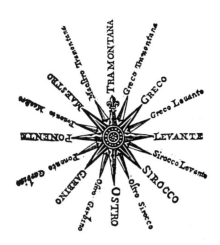

Compass roses were so-called because of their similarity to a many petalled flower. At first the points had names— different in different languages—but in A.D. 800 Charlemagne proposed that just north, south, east and west be named and all others be subdivisions of those basic four. The top figure is a compass rose from Mercator's atlas of 1635; below, a modern compass.

of fine, colored *rhumb* lines radiating from a number of large compass-roses placed centrally on the map, which connect with other smaller compasses arranged around the edges. Navigators, who did not yet have parallel rulers, could always find a line among the spidery crisscross network that was near enough to their present course to help them understand what lay ahead in any compass direction. Shorelines were crowded with the names of towns, bays, and rivers, often perched at right-angles to the coast, for the greatest economy of space. Just as Ptolemy's map outlines were copied, so were these portolan maps, which had originally been developed by Genoese sailors in the second part of the thirteenth century. Such was their accuracy that they were thought to be good enough to navigate in the Mediterranean up to the early 1600s.

Compass point names derive from the names for winds. Sailors knew directions as these names, not as points, which are numbers somewhere between 0 and 360. Every language had different names. For example, a French sailor would use the word *Levant* (literally, ''getting up'') for a wind coming from the east, and *Couchant* (''lying down'') for a wind from the west. Originally there were eight winds. Although their names differed from country to country, they corresponded to *N, NE, E, SE, S, SW, W,* and *NW*. Later, more precision was needed, and in about 800 Emperor Charlemagne introduced the 32-point wind-*rose*, so called because the overlapping colored points in the most florid examples looked like a many-petaled flower. The points that Charlemagne added were eight *half-winds* (*NNE, ENE, ESE,* etc.) and sixteen *quarter-winds* (*N* by *E, NE* by *N, NE* by *E,* etc.) At the same time, he proposed that just four winds should get names: those that blew in from the north, the east, the south, and the west. All other names were dropped to clear up confusion. The basic four could easily be translated into any language and the remaining points were to be subdivisions of them.

3. The Church   Medieval monks were not interested in scientific cartography, nor did their maps have the responsibility of steering a ship into port. Their idea of a map was a symbolic view of the world according to religious teachings. They often went back to disk maps of the sort drawn by Anaximander in 550 B.C. for reference. There was a symmetry to these round maps, and the monks pushed this to the limit, producing images simplified down to the form of a letter *T* inside an *O* (for *Orbis Terrarum*). These *T*-in-*O* maps represented the known world, but not in a literal sense. East, the Orient, was always at the top (hence *orientation*); Europe and Africa lay to the left and right of the downstroke of the *T*, which itself represented the

The Catholic church's maps of the world (right) were based on writings from the Bible, and from early disk maps, such as this one by Anaximander (550 B.C.), and from later Roman versions, in which accurate geography was ignored in favor of religious myth.

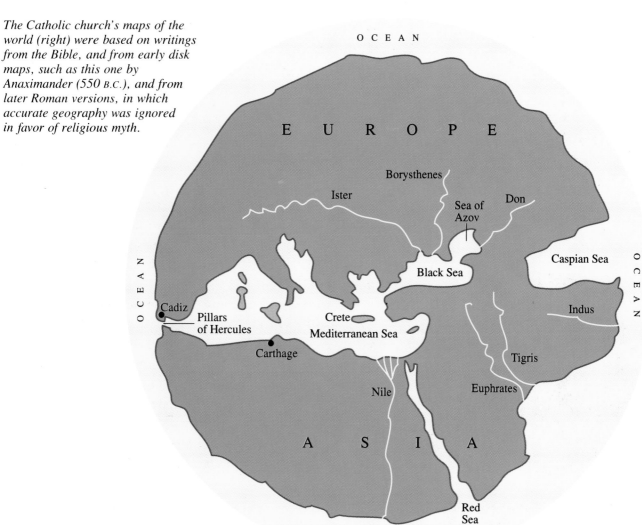

OCEAN

EUROPE

Borysthenes

Ister

Sea of Azov

Don

Black Sea

Caspian Sea

OCEAN

Cadiz

Pillars of Hercules

Crete

Mediterranean Sea

Indus

Carthage

Tigris

Nile

Euphrates

ASIA

Red Sea

OCEAN

The typical medieval world map (below) took the form of a letter T inside a letter O ("T-in-O"), with Jerusalem in the center at the top of the T.

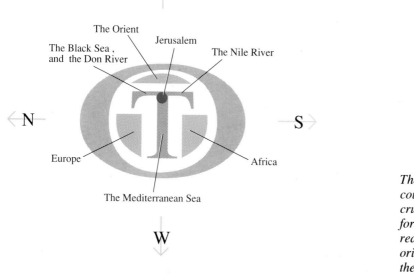

E

The Orient

Jerusalem

The Black Sea, and the Don River

The Nile River

N

S

Europe

Africa

The Mediterranean Sea

W

The T in T-in-O maps could also be read as a crucifix. This upright form was an additional reason for the church to orient maps the way they did, with east (oriens) at the top.

One of the best examples of a medieval T-in-O map is the huge Hereford world map (1290), which is filled with detail. Hidden among the more recognizable biblical references (Noah's Ark, the Garden of Eden) are monsters of all kinds: a man who shades himself from the sun with a single huge foot raised over his head, and the race that clothes itself with its own bathrobe-length ears. The map has been in Hereford Cathedral in England since at least 1682. A similar piece of medieval mapmaking was the Ebstorf map, which was destroyed in Germany in 1943. With a diameter of 13 feet, it was two-and-a-half times the size of the Hereford map, and it depicted the whole world as the body of Christ, his head, hands, and feet sticking out from the edges of the circular frame.

Detail from the Hereford map: Augustus Caesar's fashionable footwear!

Mediterranean Sea. This arrangement put Jerusalem right in the middle of the picture, and fulfilled for the monks the biblical edict: "This is Jerusalem: I have set her in the midst of the nations, and countries are round about her" (*Ezekiel* 5:5).

The *T* in *T-in-O* maps can also be read as a crucifix, which was another reason to orient the image the way they did. Some of the maps even show Christ's head sticking out at the top, two hands at the extreme left and right, and his feet at the bottom. Thus the whole world was seen to be in the form of God. Of course, churches themselves were often built on a cross plan, the four extremities facing the cardinal points of the compass.

Many *T-in-O* maps have survived. They range from small diagrams that are not much more to look at than the modern annotated version shown here, to large-scale works in which the

T and *O* structure is barely visible through the pictorial content. One of the most stunning examples of this latter group is preserved in Hereford Cathedral, where it was originally an altarpiece. The Hereford world map* was drawn by Richard of Haldingham around 1290. Glorious in its overall golden hue, it is five feet in diameter and at the top shows a figure of Christ, just above the Garden of Paradise. There are also drawings of Noah's Ark, the Tower of Babel, the Last Judgment, and masses of assorted mythological animals. Britain is squeezed in on the bottom edge, distorted to conform to the shape of the confining circle. In the border just below this is an illustration of Augustus Caesar commissioning a survey of the world from three geographers. Look at his hi-tops! Who says those guys weren't the height of fashion?

Medieval *mappaemundi* have been attacked for their lack of geographic accuracy. They have been belittled by epithets such as ''works of art, not information.'' Such criticisms miss the point, since maps of this type did not try to represent the world with geometric rectitude. Spatial relationships (one definition of a map) can be understood from all sorts of different graphic forms, and sometimes maps show relationships that are not spatial at all. There may, for example, be mental connections that need showing. Saul Steinberg's overplagiarized view of the world as seen by a New Yorker is still a *map* even though it is not plotted according to the classical rules of cartography. What worried the critics of *mappaemundi* were such statements as the one at the bottom of Matthew Paris's thirteenth century map of a somewhat stunted Britain: ''If the page had allowed it, this whole island would have been larger.'' Reading this sort of inscription did not inspire map experts to think of Paris's work as being very important to the development of their science, because their thinking was locked into a single definition. What Paris and his contemporaries did, however, was the norm for those times. They often made their work conform to the shape and size of the medium, and they deliberately set out to be symbolic. So saying that the geographic content of maps in the Middle Ages was ''impoverished and usually misleading,'' as John Wilford Noble does in his book *Mapmakers*, may represent a science-based point of view, but it cuts out any acknowledgment of a wider role for maps.

Mappaemundi can be considered important because they manage to show static geography and historical events together in

When Saul Steinberg drew the view from his studio near Ninth Avenue and made the famous cover for the March 29, 1976, issue of the New Yorker, *he had no idea that he was unleashing a classic map-image that would be ripped off by artists drawing city views around the world from Amsterdam and Paris to Princeton and Pewaukee, Wisconsin. Steinberg was rightly indignant at this copying, as he could have retired from this one piece of work had he been able to control the rights. He was also concerned that the poor quality of most of the imitations might ultimately detract from his own reputation. It now appears on anything from towels to coffee mugs.*

---

*Maps of this type were often called *mappaemundi*, after the latin *mappa*, meaning ''cloth'' or ''napkin,'' and *mundi*, ''world.'' Originally maps were drawn on cloth, so that they could be folded for traveling. The Hereford mappamundi is drawn on an animal skin. Incidentally, the word chart is from the greek *chartos*, meaning leaf of paper; because surveys and maps were recorded on sheets (whether they were skin or paper), we now use cartography as the name for the whole science.

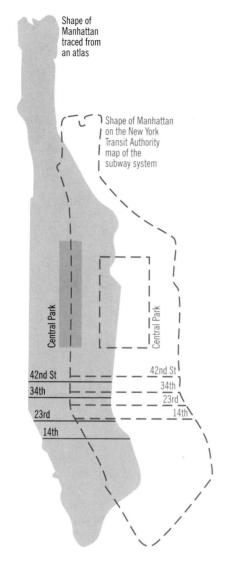

Shape of Manhattan traced from an atlas

Shape of Manhattan on the New York Transit Authority map of the subway system

Central Park

Central Park

42nd St

42nd St

34th

34th

23rd

23rd

14th

14th

By superimposing a geographically accurate map of Manhattan over the outline of the New York Transit Authority subway map, you can see how much liberty has been taken with geography in the service of graphic clarity. In the southern part of the island the width has been increased in order to include all the subway stations and to make their names legible. Meanwhile, with fewer stations in the north, the length of the island has been reduced. When you are underground you only need to know how many stops it is before you reach your destination; as a subway rider you think in terms of stops, not distance. The idea that the distance between any stop could thus be shown as one uniform distance was first exploited by Henry C. Beck in his 1933 map of the London Underground. Beck's map remains a classic, and it is a model for most transit system maps in the world today.

one picture. There is no attempt at separation. They are maps of ideas as much as of places. That they had a religious beginning and were often surrounded by church symbolism makes them an easy target for literal geographers. In his charming book about the history of communication, *From Cave Painting to Comic Strip*, Lancelot Hogben dismisses the Hereford map as ''of little interest except to the psychiatrist.'' To the critics' implied question—what use is a map if it is not accurate?—we should pose another: In exactly what respect do you mean accurate? Surely there can be accuracy in visionary, mental, and historical matters as well as in geographic.

Is the map of the New York subway system not *accurate* because the subway lines have been geographically adjusted for economy of space? The author of this map could sound like Matthew Paris in his defense of making the map fit the space. When you are traveling underground, the distance between stops is irrelevant; all you need is a straight line connecting you to your destination, and an indication of how many stops there are on the way. As with many facets of graphic design, knowing your audience is the answer to a fair study of the graphic in question.

Mercator and the Importance of Holland

All printed maps were black and white until the nineteenth century. Some were embellished with florid lettering and pictorial engraving and then hand-colored to widen their appeal and sales. The Dutch school of cartography reveled in decoration, ornament, and heraldry (unlike Italian maps which were graphically austere). At the start of the fourteenth century, Holland was a commercial center, and through artists like Ortelius and Hondius, and especially Gerhardt Kramer (1512–94), cartography developed rapidly. Frequently, scientists and other scholars adopted a latinized version of their name, and it's the Latin version of Kramer—Mercator—that is probably the most remembered name in maps.* His famous projection of 1569 (see chap. 6) is still in use today; it was drawn so that navigators could plot their routes as straight lines. Mercator even gave the *atlas* its name; he used a picture of the Greek god holding up the earth on the frontispiece of his collection of maps published in 1595, one year after his death. In the preface to this atlas, following a description of the geneology of his hero, Mercator writes: ''My purpose is to follow this *Atlas*, a man so excelling in erudition, humanity and wisdom, to contemplate cosmography as much as my strength and ability will permit me.'' The last two lines of the dedication in the English edition of 1635 read: ''Let

---

*In German *Kramer* means *trader*; the latin version actually means *world trader.* Maybe Mercator knew he was destined to help merchant mariners find their way safely to their destinations.

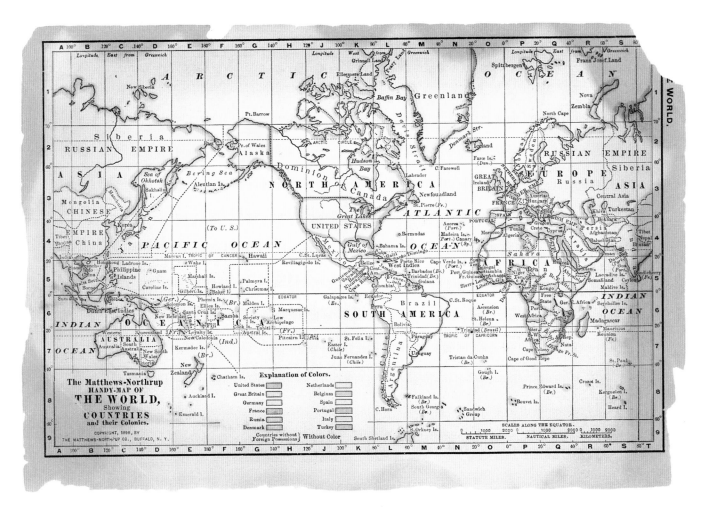

The Matthews-Northrup
HANDY-MAP OF
THE WORLD,
Showing
COUNTRIES
and their Colonies.

COPYRIGHT, 1898, BY
THE MATTHEWS-NORTHRUP CO., BUFFALO, N. Y.

Explanation of Colors.

United States		Netherlands	
Great Britain		Belgium	
Germany		Spain	
France		Portugal	
Russia		Turkey	
Denmark			

Countries without } Without Color
Foreign Possessions }

SCALES ALONG THE EQUATOR .
1000   1000   2000 0   1000   2000
STATUTE MILES.   NAUTICAL MILES.   KILOMETERS.

none henceforth be your *Mistresses* but faire *Geographie*.''

Most atlases are the collective effort of many people. Mercator, a cartographer, engraver, and calligrapher, was the exception to this. Normally a cartographer supplied drawings to an engraver, who would reproduce them and add embellishments from his own repertoire of wind-puffing cherubs, ships, monsters, and compass-roses. While Mercator did all his own mathematical drawing, then all the lettering and engraving, his commercial rival Abraham Ortelius credited dozens of different cartographers in his atlases, and they in turn had of course looked at the work of their predecessors. In the Ortelius atlas of 1603 there were contributions from 183 additional mapmakers (the ''Catalogue of Authors''). The experience of reading the list must have been not unlike sitting through the end credits of an animated cartoon feature in a movie theater today. But as John Speed, a cartographer working in England in the early years of the seventeenth century, said, ''It may be objected that I have laid my building on other men's foundations, but indeed, who can do otherwise in a subject of this nature.'' That in large part was why Mercator's achievement was so extraordinary, and his name the most remembered.

Mercator's map of the world was published in 1569 for the use of navigators. Noting both the plus and minus points of his projection, he wrote, ''If you wish to sail from one port to another, here is a chart, and a straight line on it. If you follow this line carefully you will certainly arrive at your destination. But the length of the line may not be correct. You may get there sooner or you may not get there as soon as you expected, but you will certainly get there.''

The first person to call a collection of maps an atlas, *Mercator has the name most remembered today in mapmaking. His projection lives on in school atlases, behind television news reporters, thus it is the view of the shape of the world in the minds of most people.*

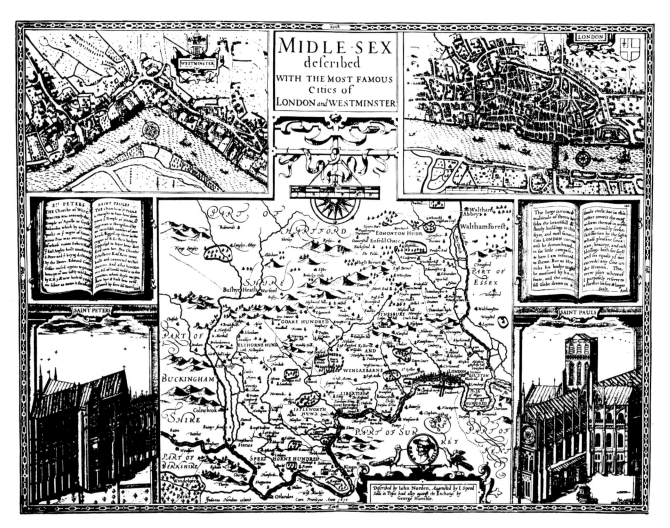

John Speed, like all cartographers, borrowed from others, most notably from Saxton and Norden. In Speed's atlas (above), Prospect of the Famous Parts of the World (1646), this led to the shapes of countries appearing differently in different parts of the atlas. He was the first cartographer to make good use of the inset town plan, and this device can be seen working very well in this map of Middlesex with closeups of the cities of London and Westminster (above). This plate is from Speed's Theatre of the Empire of Great Britaine (1612), which was the first printed atlas of the British Isles. It benefits from the beautiful and elegant handwork of the Dutch engraver Jodocus Hondius.

This is a detail of the Carta Marina, drawn by Olaus Magnus in the sixteenth century. The entire map includes Iceland, Denmark, Norway, Sweden, and Finland, and it mixes drawings and mapmaking nicely, so that the reader is entertained and informed simultaneously.

Into the Twentieth Century

I'm bringing this brief historical survey suddenly up-to-date with a look at an American artist who worked in California during the 1930s and 1940s. Jo Mora made only nine maps that were published, but they are great. Completely filled up with tiny writing and colored images from edge to edge, you can read them like a book, and take as long doing so. I met his son and daughter, Joseph and Grace, at the family home in Pebble Beach, Carmel, California. As children, their father had always drawn pictures of the daily life of the family, a sort of humorous visual diary of major and mundane events. Jo, Sr., who died in 1947, had come to the United States from Uruguay in his childhood. After an education that included some time at the Art Students' League in New York, he was taken on by the Boston *Herald* to draw their first funny pages in 1900, when he was eighteen.

Although Jo Mora's main artistic endeavor was to make heroic—and usually Western-inspired—sculptures (some of which are in the Will Rogers Memorial in Claremore, Oklahoma), his son Joseph persuaded him that the little doodles he drew to explain where the family had been would have a commercial appeal, and the son took it upon himself to be his father's publisher. The maps that resulted were of Monterey, Carmel, Pebble Beach, Los Angeles, San Diego, Yellowstone Park, the Grand Canyon, and two of California, one of which was a private commission for the Del Monte canning company (which bought the entire print-run as promotional giveaways).

Jo, Jr., showed me the artwork for the California map reproduced here and told me that his father simply sat down and drew it in one go, practically without revision. To him, art was an entirely natural occupation, whether it was drawing separated linework for a map, or painting a classical portrait in oils, or modeling a cowboy and his horse for a bronze statue. The text that entertainingly infests the maps was taken from his own knowledge of local history, and the reference for the pictures of Indian life and customs that were arranged in neat boxes around the edges was his own life: He had lived with and photographed the Hopi. What is more, the maps *were* geographically accurate, so he even managed to fulfill that contentious aspect! One graphic note that particularly struck me about Jo Mora's work is his use of black. Very bold. As a background element, he manages to use black with terrific effect in the border designs, both to show off his other colors, and to provide a heavy contrast to the necessarily lighter tones of the map areas themselves.

(Overleaf) Jo Mora's maps are a riot of color, obsessive detail, folklore, and wit. This one of the Grand Canyon (1931) has a tiny inscription at the bottom: "This remarkable birdseye phoneygraph was taken at great risk from hobbled airplane. Aint it just too natcherel for words?" For all the joking—and there are plenty of jokes—the geography of this and all of Mora's maps is precisely correct.

Jo Mora's map of California was drawn in 1945. Around the map itself he has included a wonderful collection of historical facts, beautiful little drawings of missions, humorous drawings of the "California melting pot," a graphic history of transportation from ox-drawn carts and sailboats ("That short yet glorious Clipper Ship era: N.Y. to S.F. 89 days 8 hrs.") to planes ("Giant airliners now whisk us away like the magic carpet"). At the bottom is a tribute in his own words: "I feel I may sing in all truth and sincerity 'I love you California.' . . . I've tried to make this [map] in a manner to help you keep the corners of your mouth on the up and up during the perusal."

Detail from what Jo Mora called a carte, or map of the rodeo, the history behind it, and the equipment and maneuvers that can be seen there. He uses two styles of drawing in this piece. In the rodeo arena itself are the cartoony characters familiar from his other maps. But the border decoration here is much more serious, and the detail astonishing: brands, saddles, stirrups, spurs, ropes, bridles, cattle, styles of cowboy gear, and a historical frieze of Spanish Conquistadors, through early rancheros, to regular working cowboys. Strong black fields give dramatic punch to the individual cowboy portraits, while soft pastel backgrounds allow the reader to quietly study the details.

Mora's respect for native Americans shows in this detail of a 1937 carte. Painted as a full-color original (unlike his other work, all of which was four-color separation art), this piece uses none of his humorous drawings. But like the other maps, it is crammed with details of native American artifacts, shelters, dances, costumes, rugs, and hunting equipment of different tribes. Mora spent a lot of time living with native Americans, and he won their trust. Thus his work is more than that of a well-documented traveling artist; it was endorsed by its subjects.

45

3

America

**The United States filled up with just about anything
New York City
Los Angeles and others**

All maps drawn before today can be termed *historical,* and as much can be learned from yesterday's map in the newspaper as from the Hudson Bay Eskimos, from Ptolemy, or from Mercator. But there is an important difference between then and now.

The early history of maps is the story of our developing knowledge of geography, which changed with each new piece of information added over the centuries by mathematicians, astronomers, and explorers. From now on, however, we can assume that the world is pretty well known (although I daresay we all harbor a dream of someday having enough money, time, and recklessness to go off to some uncharted isle). Cartographers today know that the world is mapped correctly, and its shorelines—though subtly changing under the erosive action of the sea—are graphically pinned down and reside comfortably in great atlases. Cartographers can and should explain, inform, amuse, and educate by building on an excellent set of base-maps.

The United States

By repetition, the shape of the map of the continental United States has entered the national collective image bank. Other icons like it are the dollar bill, George Washington's head, the bald eagle, Uncle Sam, and Old Glory. The shape of the United States is so ingrained in the minds of those who live here (and probably in the minds of a great part of the rest of the world's population, too) that it stands for the nation as a symbol.

Given a rudimentary knowledge of geography, *information* can be added to this map-image etched in our minds. Thought of as a large unit of measurement, the United States is a pretty useful standard. We can use it to gauge the size of other countries that are bigger, or to see how many smaller countries fit into it. Or we can use the unit of measurement to explain the size of something quite different. I once worked out that if all the toothpaste used daily in the United States were squeezed out in a long white line, it would be just over three thousand miles long, the width of the country. No need to even draw *that* image. It's instantly inside our heads, and unforgettable.

But back to more purely visual considerations: Here is a gallery of examples of the shape of the United States as used by all different types of designers and advertisers. What the mapmakers have in common is the simple desire to convey the impression of nationwide coverage, influence, fame, or just presence, and the map is the best way to show it. *"We are here, coast-to-coast!"* they proclaim, *"Buy us! drink us! visit our locations across the nation!"*

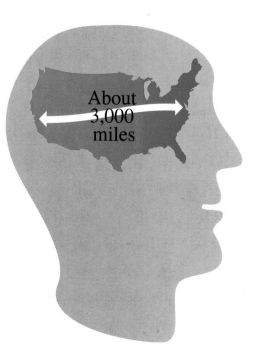

About 3,000 miles

Use the map in your mind as a template by which to judge the size of the rest of the world, or merely to visualize the 3,000-mile line of toothpaste used every day in the United States.

A 1979 advertisement for Continental Airlines divided the states into separate boxes of commodities.

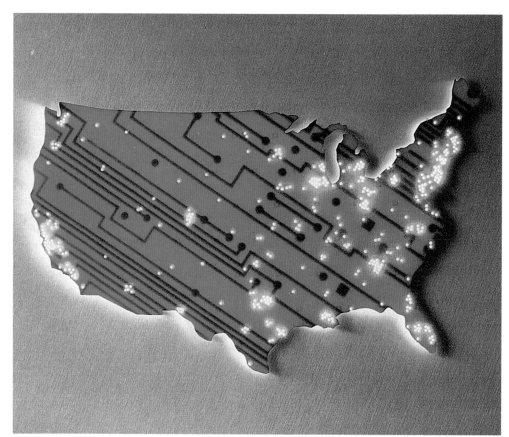

Siemens, the electronics and telecommunications company, transformed the map into a chip-like network that shows their locations from coast to coast.

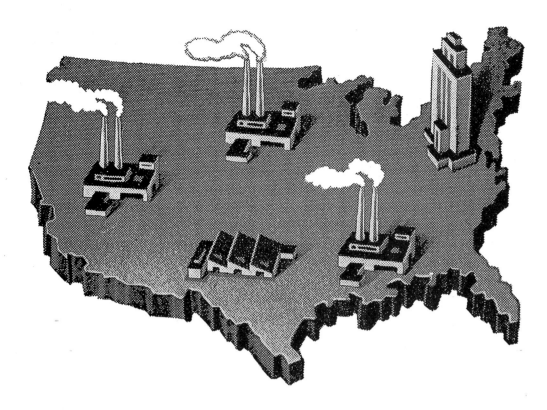

From 1977, this little map locates just a few factory sites. The land and the buildings are drawn in a very satisfactory way, unifying the map and its industrial images.

The staying power of the U.S. map-shape in our minds is such that even this simplified version, from a 1981 Movie Channel advertisement, is recognizable. The tagline to the ad says it all: "We're taking the movies to America."

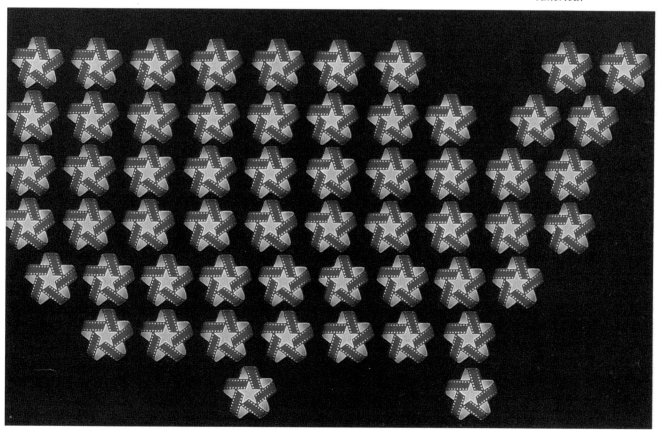

Southwestern Bell cut a yellow-pages directory into the shape of the United States for its advertisement announcing that its subsidiary Publications Division was the largest directory company in the nation: "Fingers are walking through our Yellow Pages coast-to-coast."

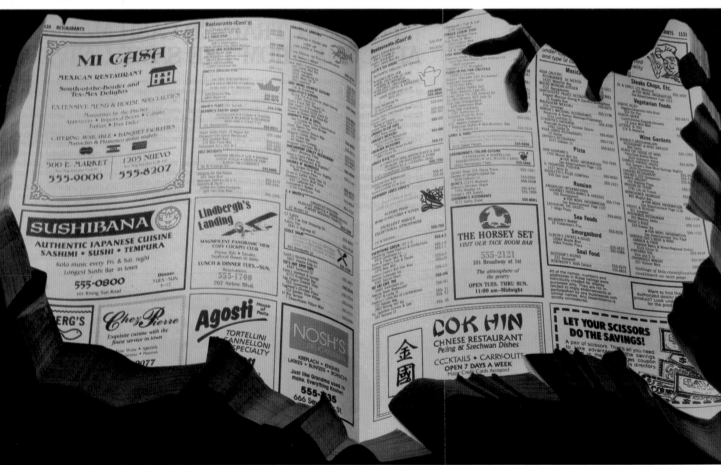

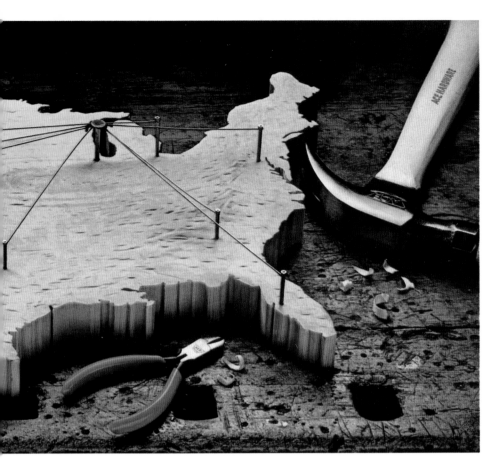

A 1982 advertisement for IBM details the success that Ace Hardware achieved when it used IBM computers to build a distributed data-processing system to link 4,000 independent retailers. As the ad says: "Ace nails down information out where it's needed."

The combination of two easily recognized symbols, the dartboard and the map, make this advertisement for the Memphis Area Chamber of Commerce ("America's Distribution Center") very effective.

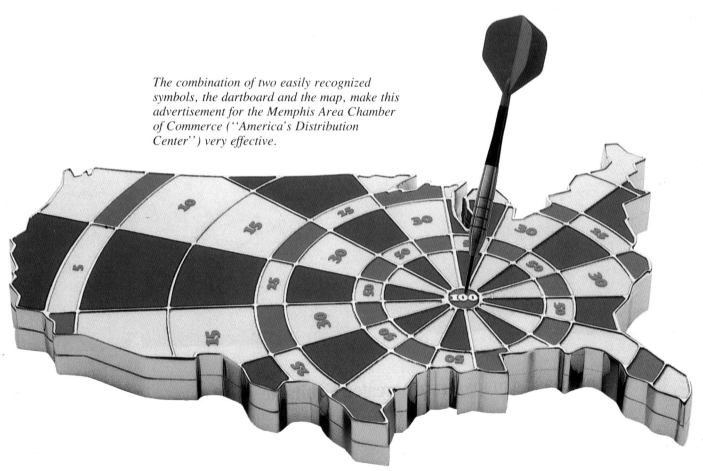

THE BOOM IN EXPEDITED DELIVERY SERVICES

This image of the states made out of packages, which appeared in the December 1982 issue of the trade magazine Zip, illustrates an article about the new crop of overnight air-delivery companies that sprang up in the early eighties.

An advertisement for the paper company, Zellerbach, with a headline about "plugging in to the right connection," confirms that the company is up-to-date, with a transcontinental network.

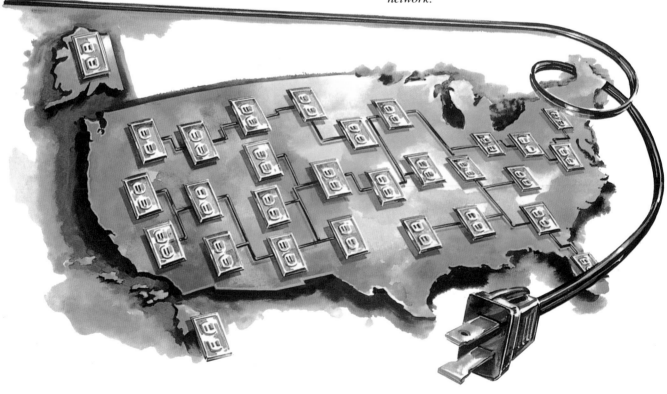

*A radio-program production company,
Westwood One, ran this piece in Adweek in
1980, informing advertisers that they would
give them ''more for their broadcast dollar.''
Thus the map is transformed into piles of cash.*

*In this advertisement for Information
Technology, cables snaking in and out of the
land-forms both enliven the map and suggest
the fast exchange of data and ideas.*

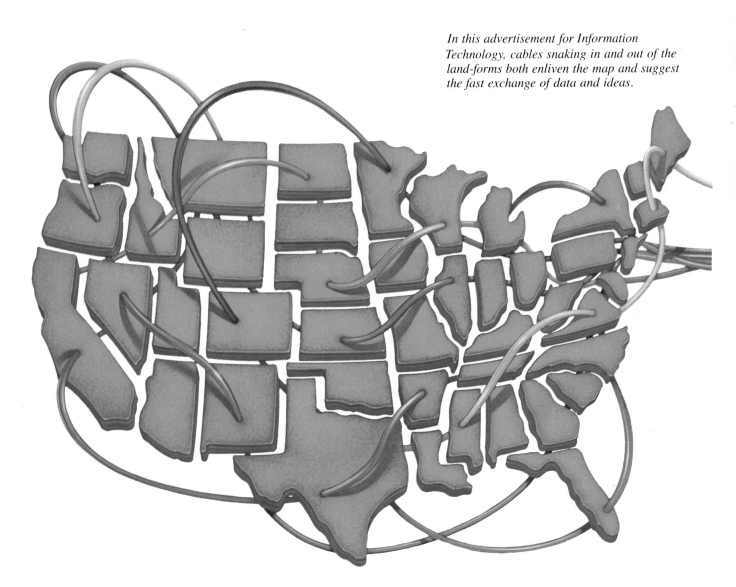

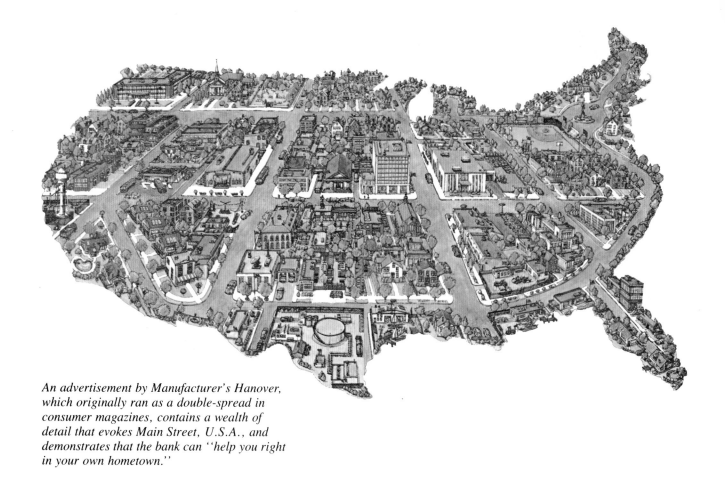

An advertisement by Manufacturer's Hanover, which originally ran as a double-spread in consumer magazines, contains a wealth of detail that evokes Main Street, U.S.A., and demonstrates that the bank can ''help you right in your own hometown.''

A different approach to a car rental ad: Hertz is proclaiming its nationwide coverage, with a fully illustrated map, the graphic opposite of the British Airways map (see p. 56).

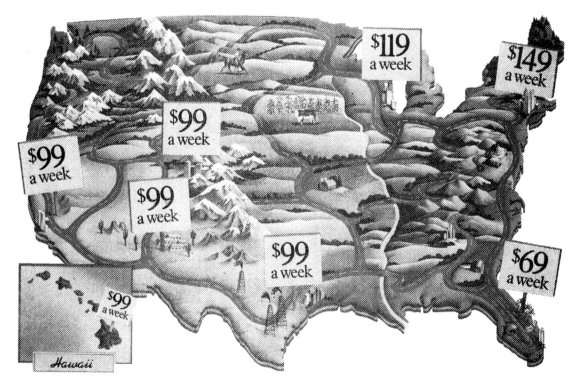

Sears's happy map with lots of cartoony detail says: "No matter where you live, travel or move in the United States, it's the only credit card that lets you say 'charge it!' . . . coast to coast." By keeping the background to a simple shoreline with no infill, the artist has kept the individual drawings from becoming a busy jumble.

This ad by the Bureau of the Census (1980), which is a good use of a photograph and well organized, exhorts us to respond to the call to be counted and optimistically fills the map with people. Note the proper inclusion of Alaska and Hawaii.

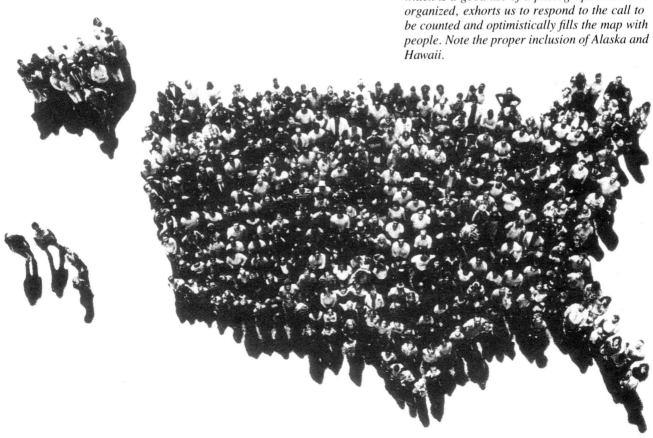

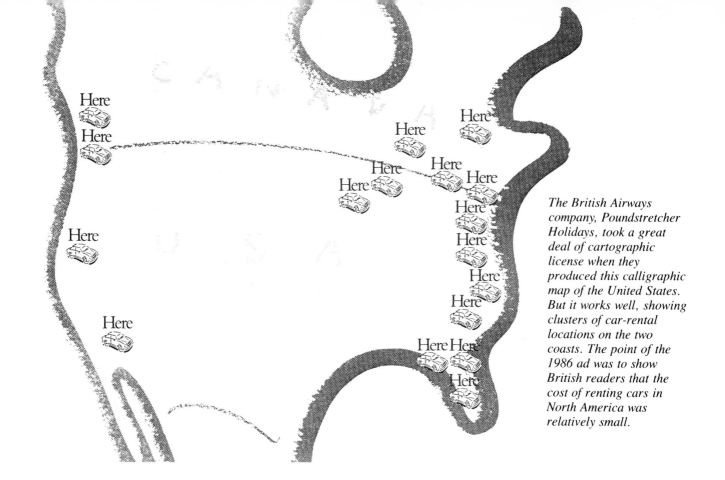

The British Airways company, Poundstretcher Holidays, took a great deal of cartographic license when they produced this calligraphic map of the United States. But it works well, showing clusters of car-rental locations on the two coasts. The point of the 1986 ad was to show British readers that the cost of renting cars in North America was relatively small.

A 1989 advertisement for Ramada trumpets their ''Great North American Sale.''

From $37. per room, per night for up to four people

This 1985 ad for Holiday Inns
wooed vacationers by
showing the whole country as
a single, inviting swimming
pool.

The British Overseas Trade
Board, advertising in
England in 1983, showed the
United States as a swimming
pool and posed the question,
"America's ready for you.
But are you ready for
America?"

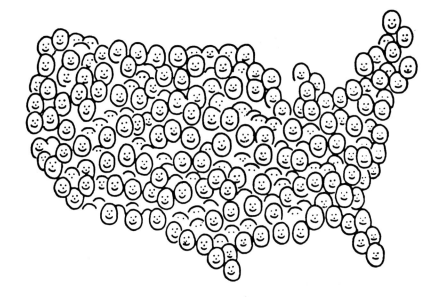

Almost falling apart in its looseness, this pleasantly casual drawing advertised a traveling computer trade show. My experience of such showcases is hardly represented by a smiling face. The smile, however, might represent the cynical amusement one experiences at the idea that any business *could be done among such packed crowds.*

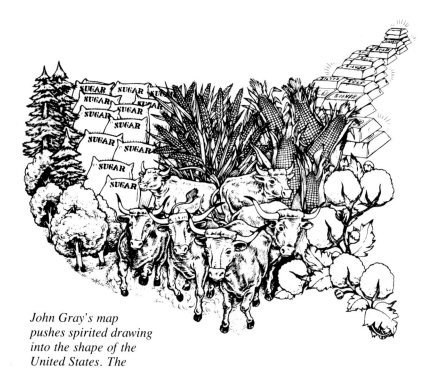

John Gray's map pushes spirited drawing into the shape of the United States. The cattle practically jump out of Texas, toward the viewer.

A map for the Port Authority entitled American Harvest *makes a good map out of food: Maine lobster, California wine, Louisiana gumbo, Georgia peaches.*

This tiny map, originally printed in a metallic silver ink with black, neatly turns an array of aluminum objects into the United States.

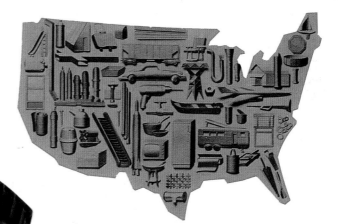

This spare outline of the United States, formed out of corrugated cardboard, encloses symbols that locate Champion International Corporation's mills and headquarters.

Telephone area code numbers are the base for this small map from a 1988 Georgia-Pacific promotion for their Hopper line of papers.

A 1985 self-promotion piece by the photographer, Avedis, makes a marvelous image with cans of red, white, and blue paint pouring into a map.

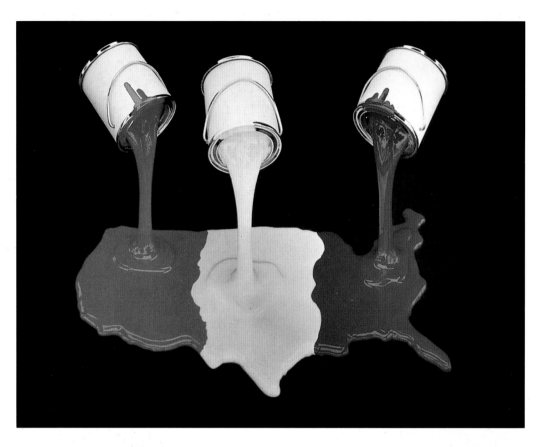

Drawn for Chicago *magazine, Roy Pendleton's wonderfully weird piece (below) about fast food is, at first sight, more illustration than map. It seems that the country is being overtaken by an invasion of tacos, much to the horror of the burger and the hot dog.*

Sports Illustrated *commissioned this terrific image (above) of American golf, which illustrated a 1990 special report about a boom in the popularity of the sport across the nation.*

Anna Walker is an illustrator whose art is exquisitely sculpted bas-reliefs. Minute pieces of precisely crafted modeling material combine to make entrancing images. This is an advertisement for EMC², a computer-memory service company.

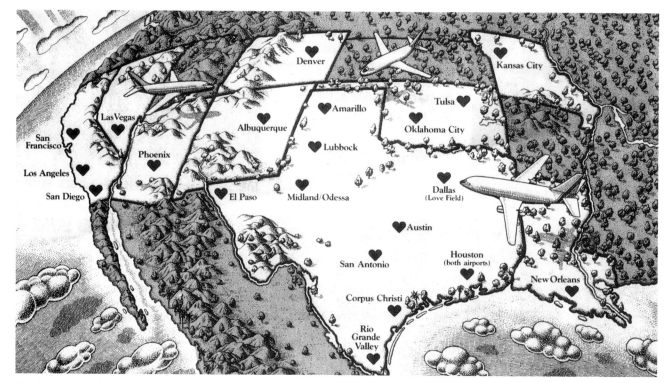

The way this beautifully rendered map for Southwest Airlines, with delicately drawn trees and clouds casting little shadows on the ground, is drawn, along with the heart-shaped symbols, follows up the theme of the advertisement—home is where the heart is—and supports the airline's claim to serve its flyers with ''genuine Southwest hospitality.''

Al Lorenz's maps are always fun to look at. Here key buildings in the country's main metropolitan areas stand tall and grab your attention.

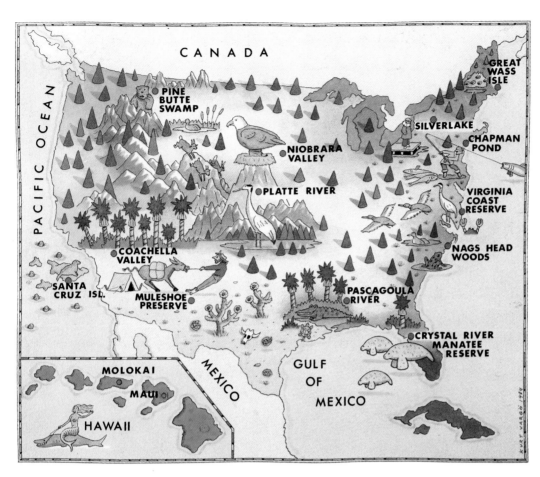

Kurt Vargo did this wildlife map for Geo magazine in 1984. Delicate watercolor washes gradually fade from one area into another, unifying the whole image.

Robert Lo Grippo's colorful panorama mixes perspective and plan in a nice pastiche of early American folk art.

Under the headline, "Win a Nation of Prizes," USA Today *ran this map announcing a competition to celebrate the newspaper's fifth anniversary.*

Mark Blanton's strong illustration style brings considerable life to this map of the United States.

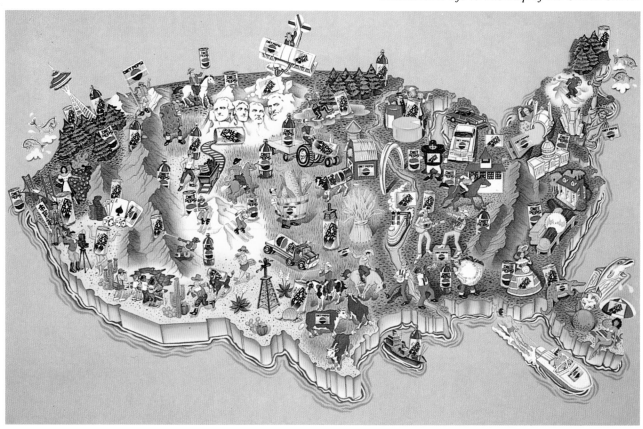

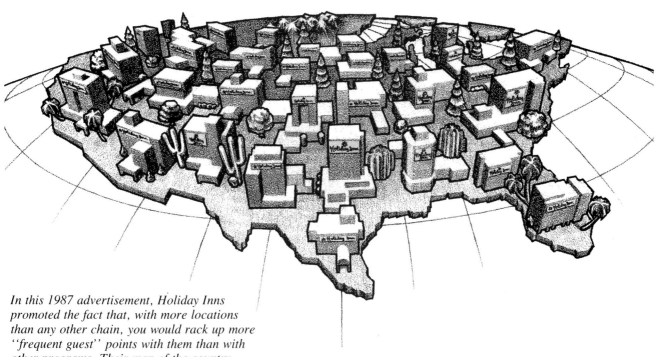

In this 1987 advertisement, Holiday Inns promoted the fact that, with more locations than any other chain, you would rack up more ''frequent guest'' points with them than with other programs. Their map of the country covered entirely with their hotels drives the point home.

Lazlo Kubinyi uses delicate penwork to achieve his effects, which are considerable. This example, for the commercial real estate company Cushman and Wakefield, nestles chunky corporate buildings into the landscape. Their apparent scale is increased by taking a viewpoint from below ground level, which defies the logic of the map's plan-view, but still works very well.

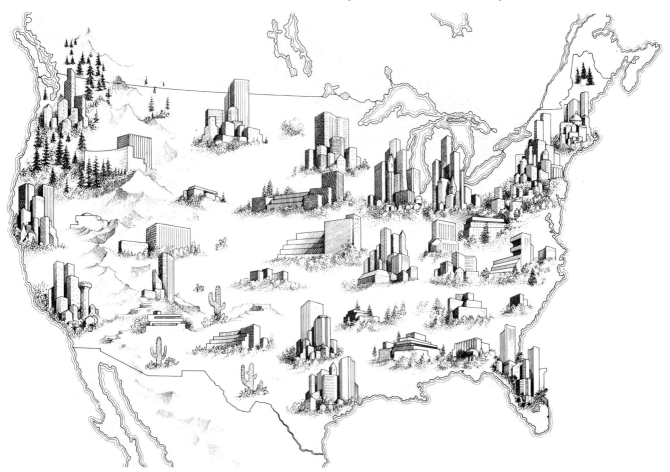

Baseball

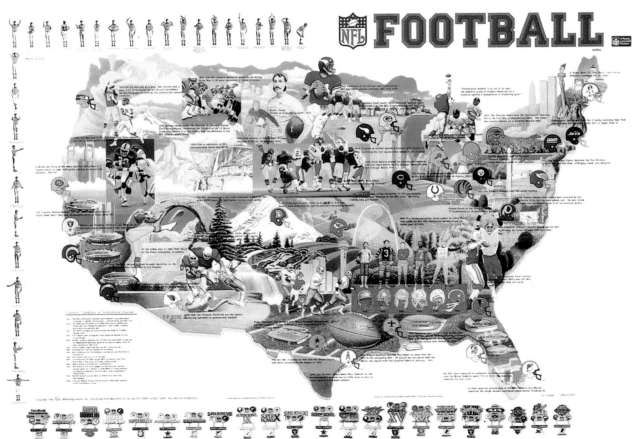

NFL FOOTBALL

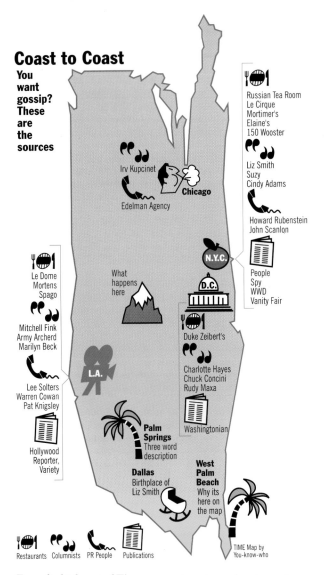

Coast to Coast

You want gossip? These are the sources

Irv Kupcinet

Edelman Agency

Chicago

Russian Tea Room
Le Cirque
Mortimer's
Elaine's
150 Wooster

Liz Smith
Suzy
Cindy Adams

Howard Rubenstein
John Scanlon

N.Y.C.

People
Spy
WWD
Vanity Fair

Le Dome
Mortens
Spago

What happens here

D.C.

Mitchell Fink
Army Archerd
Marilyn Beck

L.A.

Duke Zeibert's

Lee Solters
Warren Cowan
Pat Knigsley

Charlotte Hayes
Chuck Concini
Rudy Maxa

Hollywood Reporter, Variety

Washingtonian

Palm Springs
Three word description

Dallas
Birthplace of Liz Smith

West Palm Beach
Why its here on the map

Restaurants Columnists PR People Publications

TIME Map by You-know-who

For a light-hearted Time *magazine story about gossip (March 1990), this map pushes together the two coasts and with them the prime gossip-mongering sites. This cattily emphasizes the lack of anything very interesting going on in between New York and Los Angeles.*

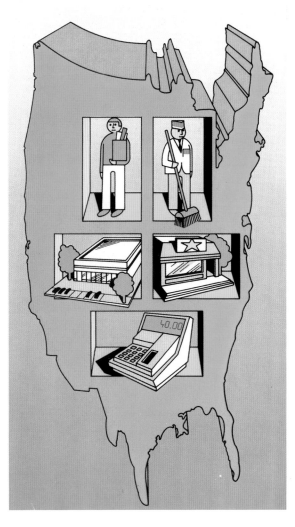

In May 1980, the trade publication Progressive Grocer *needed to squash the United States for a different reason—space. No matter; geography was not the point here. The illustration presented five aspects of the nation's supermarket business: the customer, the employee, large supermarkets, small convenience stores, and new check-out machines.*

These baseball and football maps (opposite page) of the U.S. were originally produced as large posters, but are equally powerful as postcards (from which these are reproduced). The tightly rendered paintings are full of the sort of team detail that sports fans love.

The extreme curvature of the map in this NEC advertisement intentionally makes the United States look like the whole world. The country is represented by well-known landmarks packed in until they fill the landscape from San Francisco to New York, and so close do the two coasts appear that it's easy to understand the advertiser's implied message, which is that their communications technology has actually drawn us all closer together.

Joe Lertola's best-known work is in the field of scientific diagrams. Here, for Time's business section, in 1990, he turns his talents to a relaxed map of the economic climate in various regions of the country.

Another U.S.-as-the-world image. Al Lorenz's map, anchored by bright, barbershop North and South poles, does in fact just peek over the horizon to show glimpses of the Great Wall of China, Big Ben, the Eiffel Tower, the Leaning Tower of Pisa, the Pyramids, and even the Sydney Opera House.

Joe Lertola has always challenged the technical capacity of the production department at Time *magazine. For his April 1991 map of population shifts in the United States, he used a combination of electronic tools: a three-dimensional drawing program, a photo-manipulation program, and the current industry standby program for information graphics, Illustrator 3.0. The result is a fascinating image that begs the question, ''how did he do that?''*

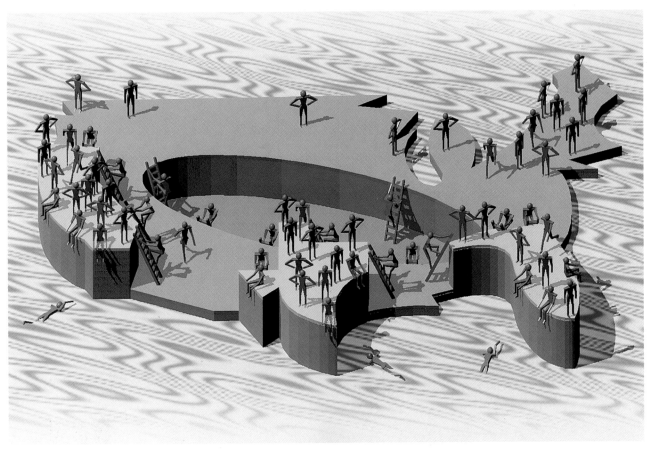

Cities

Early mapmakers' attempts at getting a clear picture of the whole world were frustrated by a lack of information. This was not true of their attempts to record their immediate surroundings. City maps were manageable because cartographers could walk the streets, measure them, and draw them. City planners could even decide what the map was going to be like before the place was built. Apart from the difference in scale between a continent and a city, the difference between nature's features and man's constructions meant that cities were always more easily recorded than those elusive shorelines.

Here is a variety of street maps that range from Rome in 1575 to Paris in 1990; from obsessively detailed views of every building in a town, to frankly decorative illustrations that attempt to convey the mood of a place as well as locations within it.

A large fold-out map with a detailed closeup of the southern tip of Manhattan (above) and of the island up to Central Park, seen from the east (below). The watercolor rendering of the key buildings, and the bird's-eye view of the city disappearing into the distance, work very well, helping visitors to understand the complexity of the place, which they may feel when walking around, but which they can't see.

Anna Walker's map of New York City neighborhoods uses background color to define median income and 3-D pictorial symbols to indicate other facts.

Less sophisticated in its execution than some of the other bird's-eye views in this chapter, this map of the PATH transit system and the connecting rail commuter lines in New York and New Jersey is nonetheless a huge step forward from the dull, purely typographic schedules that most commuters are used to seeing. A welcome move into the visual age.

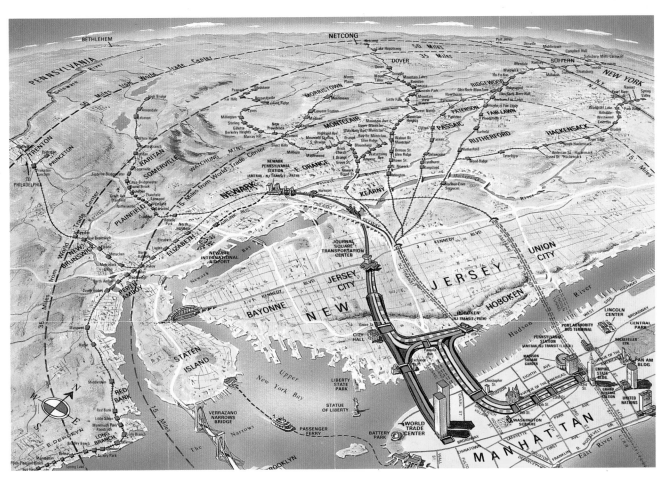

The obsessive quality of Al Lorenz's maps is compelling, and where else is it better to be obsessive if not in the rendering of hundreds of buildings? Here are three views of Manhattan by him. The opposite two show how you can use the same base but highlight different structures. To emphasize lower Manhattan, Lorenz has swung round to view the island from the south, allowing perspective to fade out the image in the north (above).

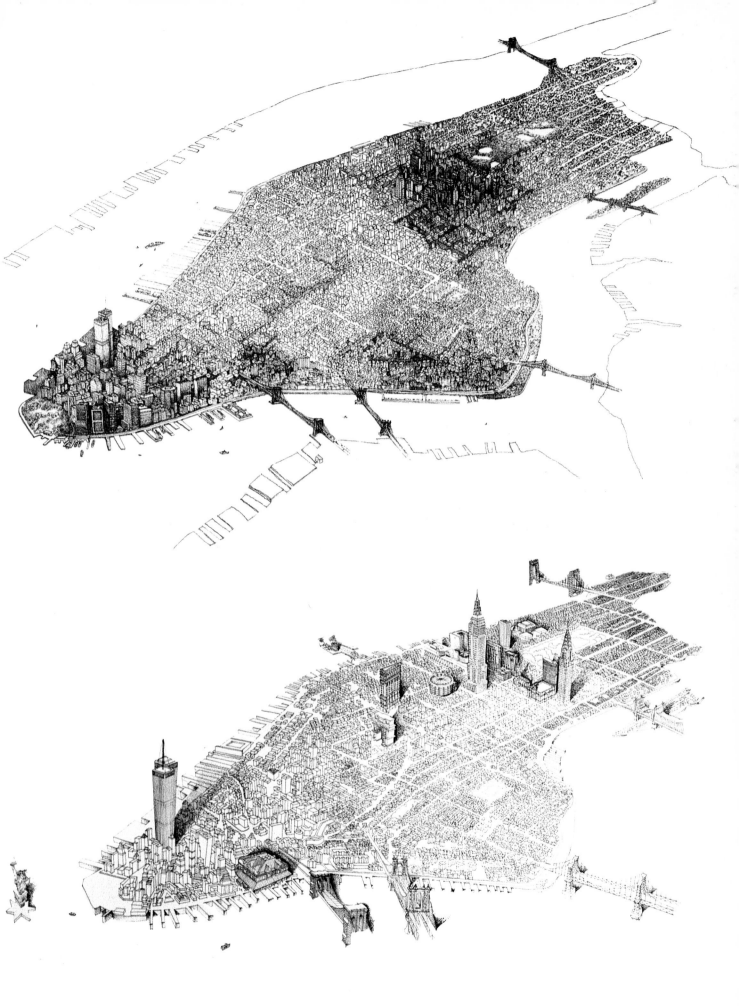

73

REGULAR GUY MANHATTAN

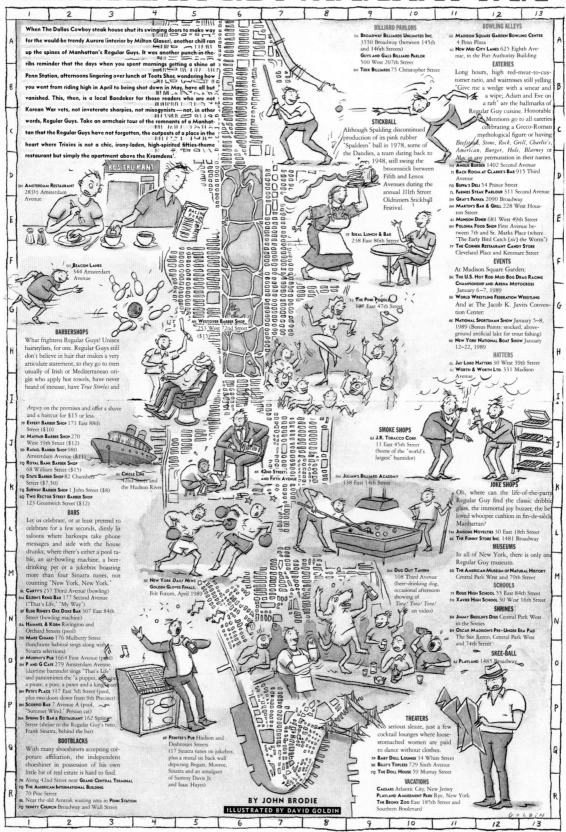

When The Dallas Cowboy steak house shut its swinging doors to make way for the would-be trendy Aurora (interior by Milton Glaser), another chill ran up the spines of Manhattan's Regular Guys. It was another punch-in-the-ribs reminder that the days when you spent mornings getting a shine at Penn Station, afternoons lingering over lunch at Toots Shor, wondering how you went from riding high in April to being shot down in May, have all but vanished. This, then, is a local Baedeker for those readers who are not Korean War vets, not inveterate sharpies, not misogynists—not, in other words, Regular Guys. Take an armchair tour of the remnants of a Manhattan that the Regular Guys have not forgotten, the outposts of a place in the heart where Trixies is not a chic, irony-laden, high-spirited fifties-theme restaurant but simply the apartment above the Kramdens'.

5H AMSTERDAM RESTAURANT 283½ Amsterdam Avenue

3G BEACON LANES 344 Amsterdam Avenue

BARBERSHOPS

What frightens Regular Guys? Unisex hairstylists, for one. Regular Guys still don't believe in hair that makes a very articulate statement, so they go to men usually of Irish or Mediterranean origin who apply hot towels, have never heard of mousse, have *True Stories* and *Argosy* on the premises and offer a shave and a haircut for $15 or less.

7F EXPERT BARBER SHOP 171 East 88th Street ($10)

5K MAYFAIR BARBER SHOP 270 West 39th Street ($12)

5D RAFAEL BARBER SHOP 980 Amsterdam Avenue ($11)

7Q ROYAL BANK BARBER SHOP 68 William Street ($15)

7Q STATE BARBER SHOP 82 Chambers Street ($7.50)

7Q SUBWAY BARBER SHOP 1 John Street ($8)

6Q TWO RECTOR STREET BARBER SHOP 123 Greenwich Street ($12)

BARS

Let us celebrate, or at least pretend to celebrate for a few seconds, dimly lit saloons where barkeeps take phone messages and side with the house drunks; where there's either a pool table, an air-bowling machine, a beer-drinking pet or a jukebox boasting more than four Sinatra tunes, not counting "New York, New York."

8L CARTY'S 257 Third Avenue (bowling)

8M EILEEN'S RENO BAR 177 Second Avenue ("That's Life," "My Way")

8F ELSIE RENEE'S OKE DOKE BAR 307 East 84th Street (bowling machine)

8A HAMMEL & KORN Rivington and Orchard Streets (pool)

7O MARE CHIARO 176 Mulberry Street (lunchtime habitué sings along with Sinatra selections)

8F MURPHY'S PUB 1664 First Avenue (pool)

5H P AND G CAFE 279 Amsterdam Avenue (daytime bartender sings "That's Life" and pantomimes the "a puppet, a pauper, a pirate, a poet, a pawn and a king" part)

8N PETE'S PLACE 317 East 5th Street (pool, plus two doors down from 9th Precinct)

8P SCORPIO BAR 7 Avenue A (pool, "Summer Wind," Persian cat)

8M SPRING ST. BAR & RESTAURANT 162 Spring Street (shrine to the Regular Guy's hero, Frank Sinatra, behind the bar)

BOOTBLACKS

With many shoeshiners accepting corporate affiliation, the independent shoeshiner in possession of his own little bit of real estate is hard to find.

7K Along 42nd Street near GRAND CENTRAL TERMINAL

7Q THE AMERICAN INTERNATIONAL BUILDING 70 Pine Street

8L Near the old Amtrak waiting area in PENN STATION

7Q TRINITY CHURCH Broadway and Wall Street

6P PRINTER'S PUB Hudson and Desbrosses Streets (17 Sinatra tunes on jukebox, plus a mural on back wall depicting Bogart, Monroe, Sinatra and an amalgam of Sammy Davis Jr. and Isaac Hayes)

BILLIARD PARLORS

5A BROADWAY BILLIARDS UNLIMITED INC. 3550 Broadway (between 145th and 146th Streets)

GUYS AND GALS BILLIARD PARLOR 500 West 207th Street

6H TEKK BILLIARDS 75 Christopher Street

STICKBALL

Although Spalding discontinued production of its pink rubber "Spaldeen" ball in 1978, some of the Dandies, a team dating back to 1948, still swing the broomstick between Fifth and Lenox Avenues during the annual 111th Street Oldtimers Stickball Festival.

7F IDEAL LUNCH & BAR 238 East 86th Street

7J THE PINK POODLE 127 East 47th Street

6H WESTOVER BARBER SHOP 253 West 72nd Street ($15)

4J CIRCLE LINE 42nd Street and the Hudson River

6K 42ND STREET AND FIFTH AVENUE

6J J.R. TOBACCO CORP. 11 East 45th Street (home of the "world's largest" humidor)

SMOKE SHOPS

8M JULIAN'S BILLIARD ACADEMY 138 East 14th Street

5K NEW YORK DAILY NEWS GOLDEN GLOVES FINALS Felt Forum, April 1989)

8M DUG OUT TAVERN 108 Third Avenue (beer-drinking dog, occasional afternoon showing of *Tora! Tora! Tora!* on video)

BOWLING ALLEYS

6K MADISON SQUARE GARDEN BOWLING CENTER 4 Penn Plaza

6J NEW MID CITY LANES 625 Eighth Avenue, in the Port Authority Building

EATERIES

Long hours, high red-meat-to-customer ratio, and waitresses still yelling "Give me a wedge with a smear and a wipe; Adam and Eve on a raft" are the hallmarks of Regular Guy cuisine. Honorable Mentions go to all eateries celebrating a Greco-Roman mythological figure or having *Beefsteak, Stone, Rock, Grill, Charlie's, American, Burger, Hole, Blarney* or *Mac* in any permutation in their names.

7H ANGUS BURGER 1402 Second Avenue

7J BACK ROOM at CLARKE'S BAR 915 Third Avenue

7O BUFFA'S DELI 54 Prince Street

7L FARNES STEAK PARLOUR 311 Second Avenue

5H GRAY'S PAPAYA 2090 Broadway

6M MARTIN'S BAR & GRILL 228 West Houston Street

4J MUNSON DINER 681 West 49th Street

8N POLONIA FOOD SHOP First Avenue between 7th and St. Marks Place (where "The Early Bird Catch [*sic*] the Worm")

7P THE CORNER RESTAURANT CANDY STORE Cleveland Place and Kenmare Street

EVENTS

At Madison Square Garden:

6K THE U.S. HOT ROD MUD BOG DRAG RACING CHAMPIONSHIP AND ARENA MOTOCROSS January 6–7, 1989

5K WORLD WRESTLING FEDERATION WRESTLING

And at The Jacob K. Javits Convention Center:

4K NATIONAL SPORTSMAN SHOW January 5–8, 1989 (Bonus Points: stocked, above-ground artificial lake for trout fishing)

4K NEW YORK NATIONAL BOAT SHOW January 12–22, 1989

HATTERS

6L JAY LORD HATTERS 30 West 39th Street

6J WORTH & WORTH LTD. 331 Madison Avenue

JOKE SHOPS

Oh, where can the life-of-the-party Regular Guy find the classic dribble glass, the immortal joy buzzer, the beloved whoopee cushion in fin-de-siècle Manhattan?

7M JIMSONS NOVELTIES 30 East 18th Street

6K THE FUNNY STORE INC. 1481 Broadway

MUSEUMS

In all of New York, there is only one Regular Guy museum.

5O THE AMERICAN MUSEUM OF NATURAL HISTORY Central Park West and 79th Street

SCHOOLS

7J REGIS HIGH SCHOOL 55 East 84th Street

7H XAVIER HIGH SCHOOL 30 West 16th Street

SHRINES

5H JIMMY BRESLIN'S DIGS Central Park West in the Sixties

6J OSCAR MADISON'S PRE-UNGER ERA PAD The San Remo, Central Park West and 74th Street

SKEE-BALL

6J PLAYLAND 1485 Broadway

THEATERS

No serious sleaze, just a few cocktail lounges where loose-stomached women are paid to dance without clothes.

7P BABY DOLL LOUNGE 34 White Street

5K BILLY'S TOPLESS 729 Sixth Avenue

7Q THE DOLL HOUSE 59 Murray Street

VACATIONS

CAESARS Atlantic City, New Jersey

PLAYLAND AMUSEMENT PARK Rye, New York

THE BRONX ZOO East 185th Street and Southern Boulevard

BY JOHN BRODIE

ILLUSTRATED BY DAVID GOLDIN

GOLDIN

Spy magazine treats maps as a wonderful excuse to use lively illustrations of different facets of New York City Life. This one, by David Goldin, is their ''Regular Guy'' map, which ran in the October 1988 issue.

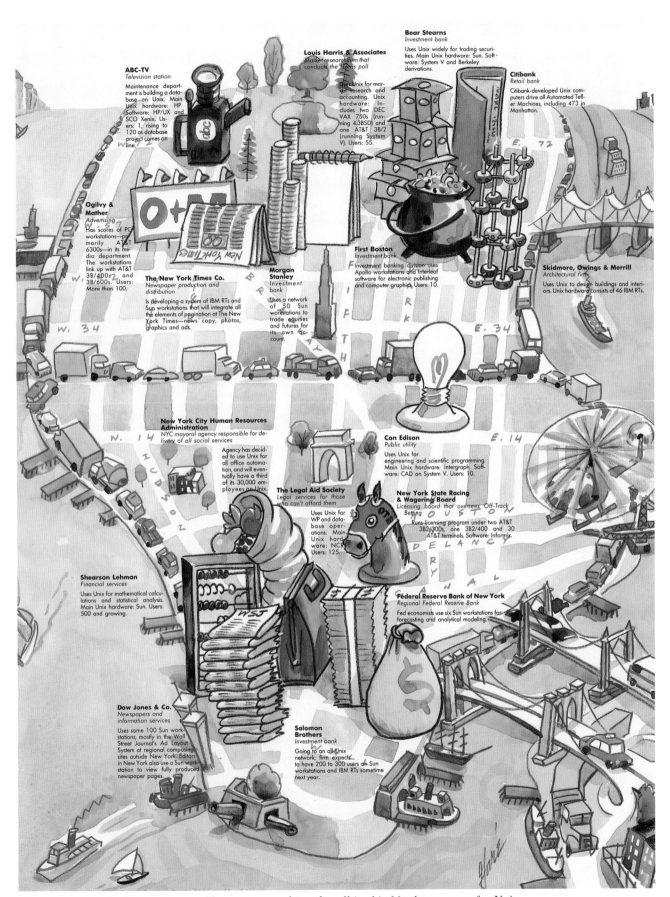

Illustrator Gary Hallgren's sense of humor comes through well in this Manhattan map for Unix.

This funny drawing of downtown Manhattan by Wallop Manyum, for Departures *magazine bristles with activity.*

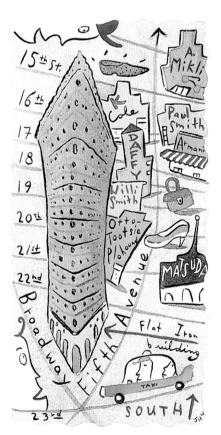

A simple view of lower Fifth Avenue by Jessie Hartland, from Departures *magazine. The peculiarity of the Flatiron Building, actually one of the city's most beautiful early skyscrapers, is well captured in this charming map.*

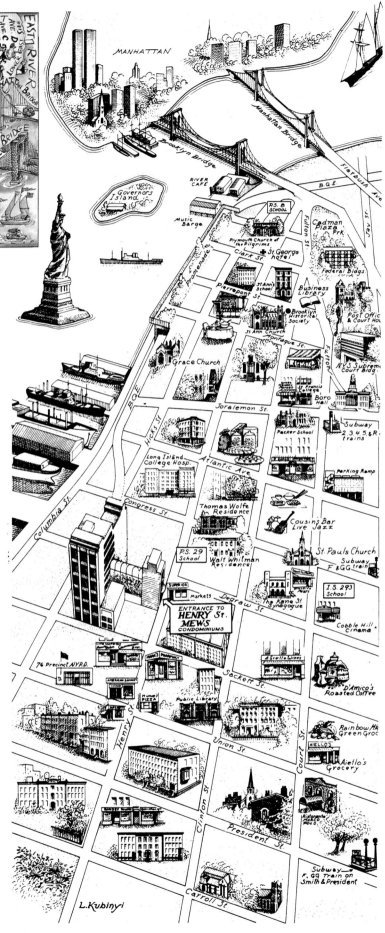

EAST
RIVER

(Left) This is from a prospectus for the Henry Street Condos in Brooklyn. Laszlo Kubinyi's light touch makes this a really friendly piece of information graphics. It's proof that you don't always need glorious full-color. Sometimes a simple black-and-white pen-and-ink drawing gives a more human feel to the architecture and the surrounding neighborhood.

This famous map of midtown Manhattan is by far the best example of a completely accurate picture of a city's structures to be found anywhere in cartography today. It was composed after the artist first viewed two sorts of aerial photographs: those looking down at the ground at 90 degrees and those looking down obliquely at 45 degrees. Next, the artist had to consult photos taken at street level. Armed with this reference, together with architects' plans, the painstaking work of drawing all the buildings began (there may be anywhere from one to forty buildings filling a single city block). The streets had to be widened a little so that not too much was obscured by the buildings in front of them, and of course the perspective in the photographs had to be constantly corrected into an axonometric projection. The drawing was begun in 1961 by Constantine Anderson, and updated by him until 1981. Since then, the architectural firm of Allon, Ryzinski and Martinez has added more than sixty buildings to make the map current up to 1985. The restricted use of color adds to the authoritative tone of the piece.

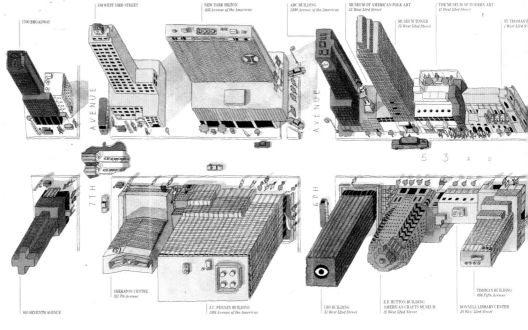

Steve Guarnaccia's map for the Museum of Modern Art is delightful. His funny drawings have graced the pages of hundreds of magazines, as well as his own books. Here, his visual wit is perfectly in tune with the subject matter.

The 1990 New York Marathon as seen by illustrator Tom Bloom. The annual event attracts thousands of participants and hundreds of thousands of spectators. In this compact map of the route, Bloom manages to show the roads and have a lot of fun, too.

It took artist Joan Steiner four months to make and assemble the roughly one thousand pieces in this magnificent three-dimensional map (right) for the 1984 New York Marathon. The panorama is five feet wide and was constructed expressly for the camera: In reality, the back is wider than the front. This compensates for the distortion that occurs when photographing such a piece. Here everything stands up straight and remains in focus.

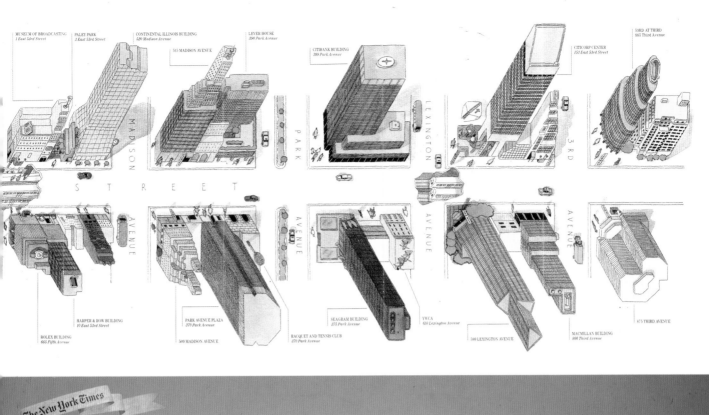

This guide to Pelham Bay Park was designed
and illustrated by Jean Wisenbaugh in 1988.
Copies of the map with "you are here" markers
are situated in the park. The bright color
scheme and nicely simplified drawings of all the
activities help visitors find their way around.

*In his 1989 map of Connecticut and part of
New York State for a System 1 advertisement,
Randall Enos uses his linocut technique not
only for the energetic real-estate salespeople
showing properties to prospective buyers, but
also for the blue-and-white town nameplates.
By rendering all the information—art and
type—with the same hand, he unifies the image
very effectively. Note the witty compass.*

This, and the following four maps of areas in Los Angeles, are from Fifty Maps of L.A. *(1991) by Istvan Banyai. Rather more illustration than map in this example, but great fun. As well as noting all the places that bikers hang out, one of the sites marked is Cedars-Sinai Medical Center, where you can go for surgery after that bad accident.*

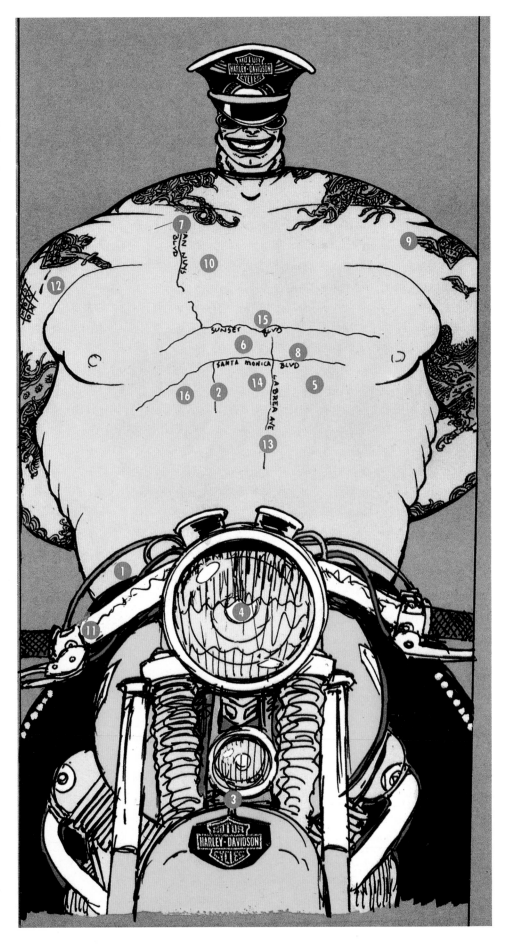

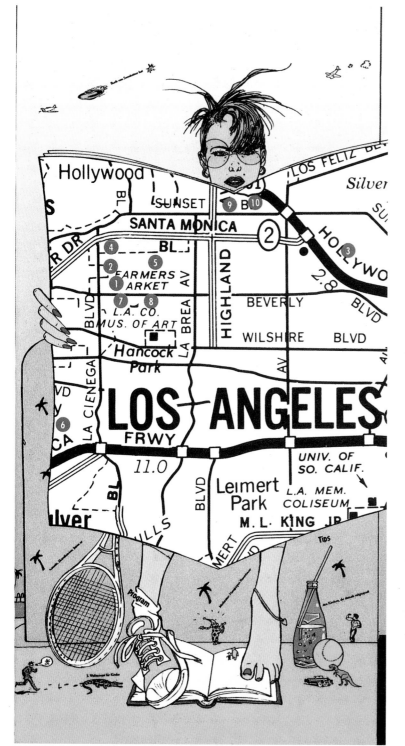

Dripping oil delineates the coastline from the Ventura county line in the north to Long Beach and beyond in the south for a map of ecological Los Angeles. Locations are shown for both offenders (the Westwood campus of UCLA is noted for using more water than anyone or anything in Los Angeles) and crusaders (such as the Buy-Back Center: recycle and get paid for your stuff, too).

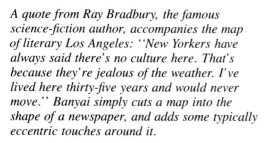

A quote from Ray Bradbury, the famous science-fiction author, accompanies the map of literary Los Angeles: ''New Yorkers have always said there's no culture here. That's because they're jealous of the weather. I've lived here thirty-five years and would never move.'' Banyai simply cuts a map into the shape of a newspaper, and adds some typically eccentric touches around it.

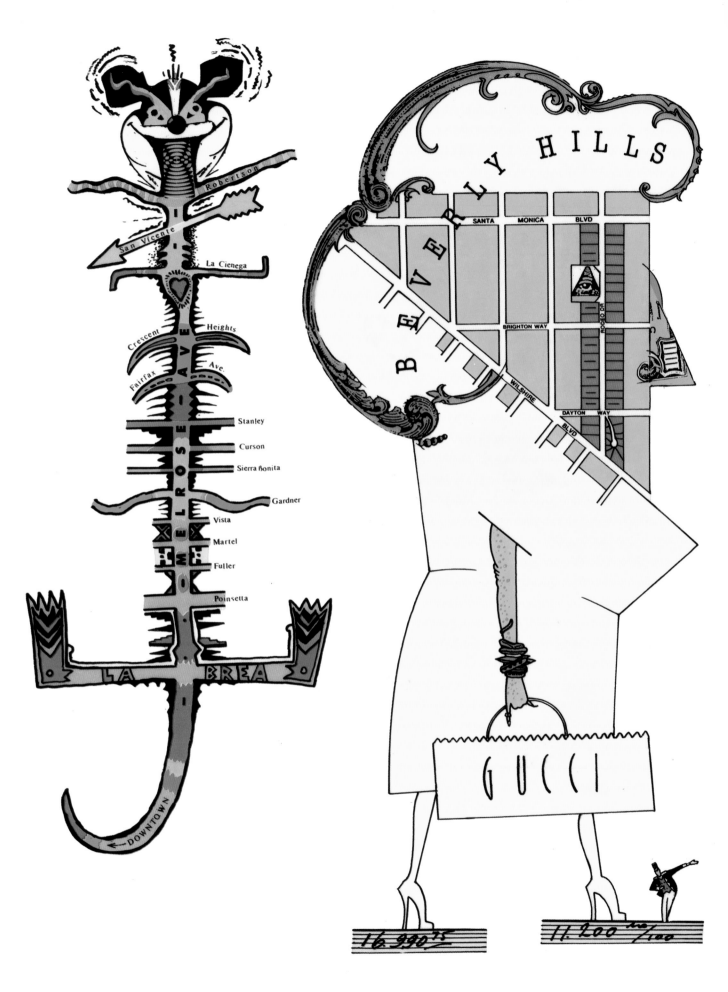

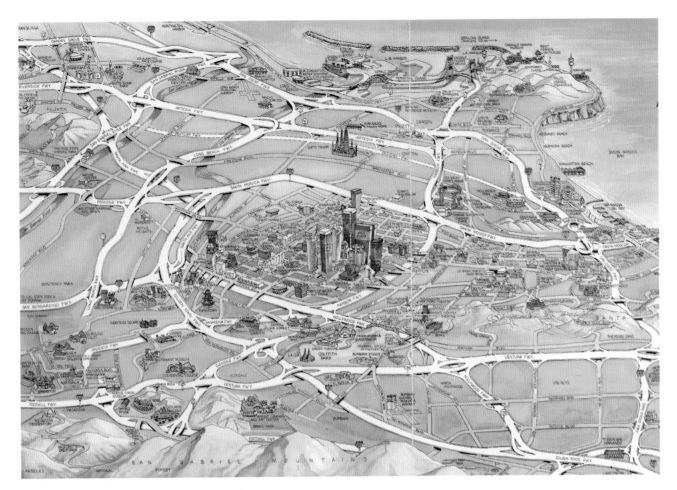

It's the choice of viewpoint—south is at the top—that distinguishes this 1983 map of Los Angeles from others. It was drawn by Swaena Lavelle of Unique Media, for Atlantic Richfield, to celebrate the 1984 Olympic Games. Although it is not drawn to scale, the simple reversal of orientation forces the viewer to read the city differently.

(Far left) Banyai uses Melrose Avenue as the backbone for an odd Mexican Mouse. The artist's hot combination of colors really sings.

The map on the left is ''Zsa Zsa's walking tour of Rodeo Drive.'' Istvan Banyai's angular and quirky style of drawing fits well with maps. This example is a good marriage of imaginative illustration and information.

Four tiny maps that originally appeared on different pages of a brochure about the Anaheim area of Los Angeles. Disneyland is the obvious reason for most visitors to be there, so these four stores all used the same map in their advertisements to show where they were located relative to the famous park.

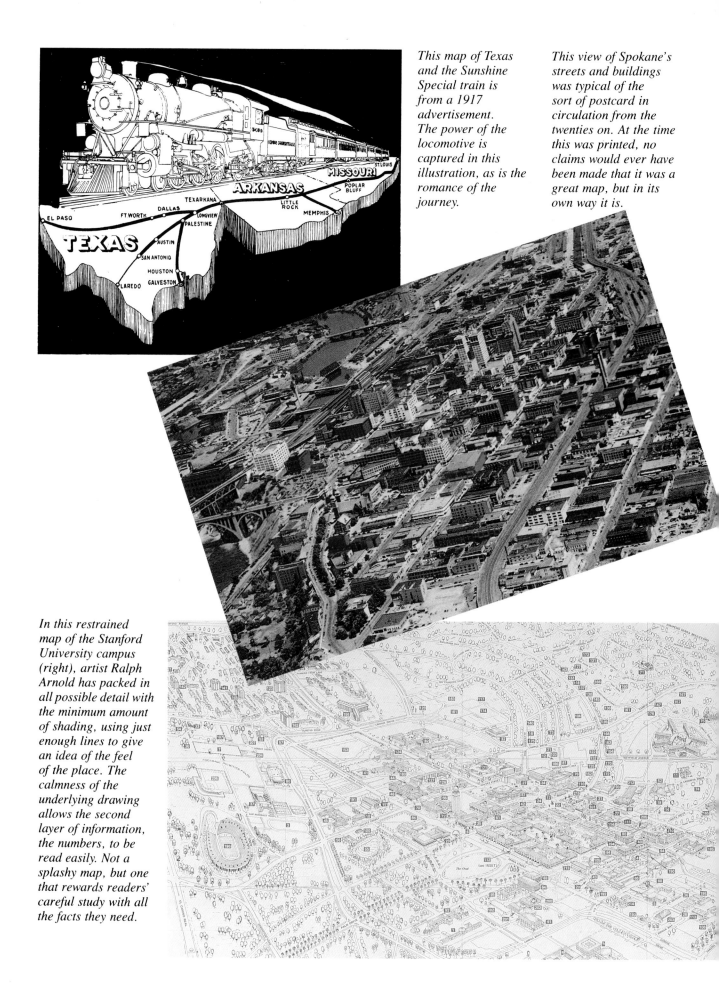

This map of Texas and the Sunshine Special train is from a 1917 advertisement. The power of the locomotive is captured in this illustration, as is the romance of the journey.

This view of Spokane's streets and buildings was typical of the sort of postcard in circulation from the twenties on. At the time this was printed, no claims would ever have been made that it was a great map, but in its own way it is.

In this restrained map of the Stanford University campus (right), artist Ralph Arnold has packed in all possible detail with the minimum amount of shading, using just enough lines to give an idea of the feel of the place. The calmness of the underlying drawing allows the second layer of information, the numbers, to be read easily. Not a splashy map, but one that rewards readers' careful study with all the facts they need.

At the start of Ronald Reagan's second term in office, in 1985, USA Today ran this full-page map of the inauguration parade route, from the swearing in by the Capitol to the White House. Web Bryant's drawings capture the essence of the architecture along the way despite an unconventional change of perspective around Thirteenth Street.

Greetings from WASHINGTON

Greetings from OREGON

Greetings from IDAHO

BIG SKY COUNTRY

MONTANA

NORTH DAKOTA

MINNESOTA

Greetings from CALIFORNIA

Greetings from NEVADA

Greetings from UTAH

Greetings from

South Dakota

IOWA

COLORADO

NEBRASKA

Greetings from MISSOURI

Hawaiian Islands

ARIZONA
Land of the Sun

INTERSTATE 40 THRU...
New Mexico

Greetings from KANSAS

MISSISSIPPI

INDIAN TERRITORY
OKLAHOMA

Greetings from
ARKANSAS

Greetings from Texas

The Lone Star State

This is Historical
Louisiana
The Bayou State

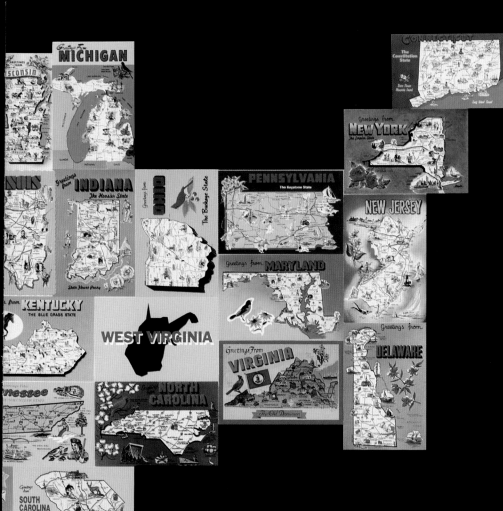

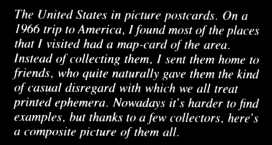

The United States in picture postcards. On a 1966 trip to America, I found most of the places that I visited had a map-card of the area. Instead of collecting them, I sent them home to friends, who quite naturally gave them the kind of casual disregard with which we all treat printed ephemera. Nowadays it's harder to find examples, but thanks to a few collectors, here's a composite picture of them all.

4

World

**The whole earth picture, then smaller bits
Streetmaps from all over**

Just as the map of the United States stands for the nation as a symbol, and on a commercial level indicates national coverage of a product or service, so it is with the world. *Worldwide coverage, international cooperation,* and *global representation* can all be symbolized by a globe, which does not even have to have any land on it. A simple circle with crisscrossing lines on it is sufficient. This is the ultimate map: only the framework is left, like a skeleton without flesh and bones.

This chapter shows views of the world in advertisements, illustrations, informative diagrams, and travel maps. There are, as with maps of the United States, as many different approaches as there are topics.

The map of the world is so familiar to most people that extreme liberties can be taken with it in the service of illustration. Once released from the responsibility of having to get someone from A to B, the shapes of the world's countries can be drawn as clouds, classical sculptures, buttons or musical instruments (see pages 93–94, 98–99). Advertisers know the potency of the world-as-symbol, and precisely *because* they are not giving directions, advertiser's maps are among the most inventive of all illustrative pictorial maps and the farthest from those on the pages of our schoolbook atlases.

Advertiser's maps can be precise as well as creative. Every destination is clearly shown on the China Airlines route map (see page 94). And the wine map of the world is quite informative. Think about the reference that preceded such a map on the artist's drawing board. It was probably very dull. The resulting map, however, invites you in to read it. It entertains you, *and* it delivers the information. It's not just a pretty face.

Todd Schorr's November 1982 Time *cover about the economic upswing in Asia makes an immaculately airbrushed globe into a face with a smiling fever-graph mouth.*

A tiny drawing by Richard Bennett from the New York Times, *1990— how little you need to recognize the world'*

An advertisement (above) for SAP, a software company specializing in the worldwide integration of all aspects of a business. Their image takes a dissembled globe and reconstructs it, illustrating the advantage of a clear global picture over a jumbled one.

A seriously distorted earth, from the June 1983 issue of Esquire *magazine, illustrating how small the world can become in the hands of a clever telephone-service thief.*

This intriguing piece of sculptural illustration by Meredith Bergman was privately commissioned by a journalist who travels all over the world in the course of her work. Bergman used many devices to create this map, including clouds to represent Europe through the Far East, the top of a tree for North and Central America, and "gallery-mounted" sculptures for Australia, South America, and Africa.

A brilliant advertisement for KLM, showing the world as a cloudscape.

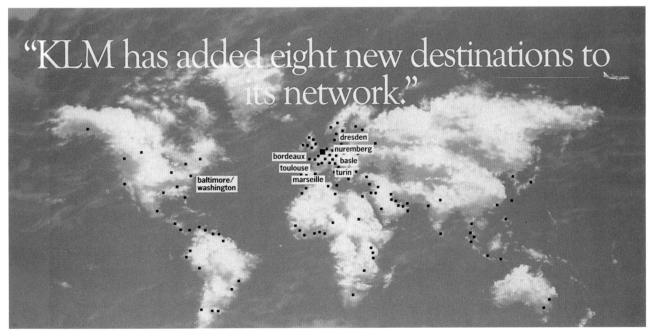

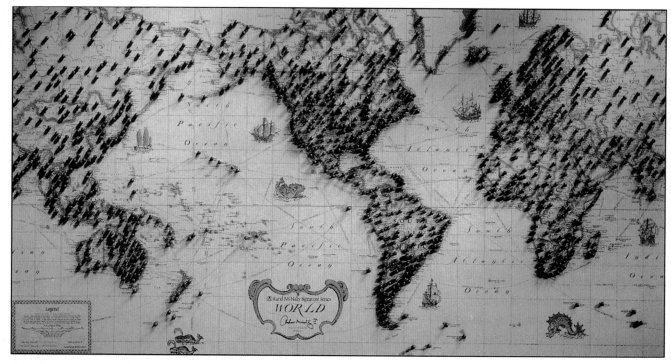

A 1990 advertisement for Visa uses pins to show the locations of over seven million places around the world where this credit card is accepted.

"With China Airlines, you've got the whole world buttoned up" is the headline to this whimsical but informative advertising map of CAL routes.

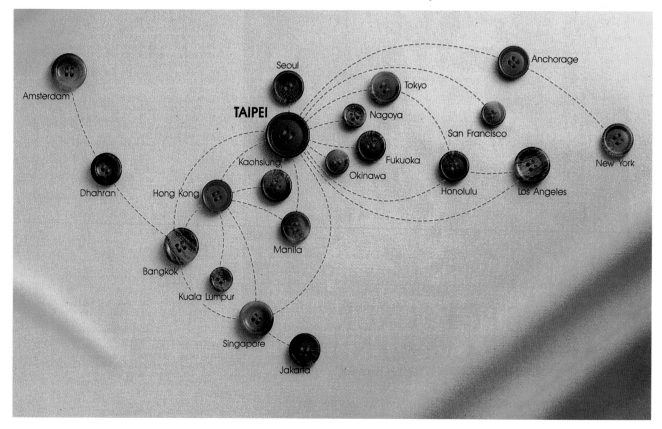

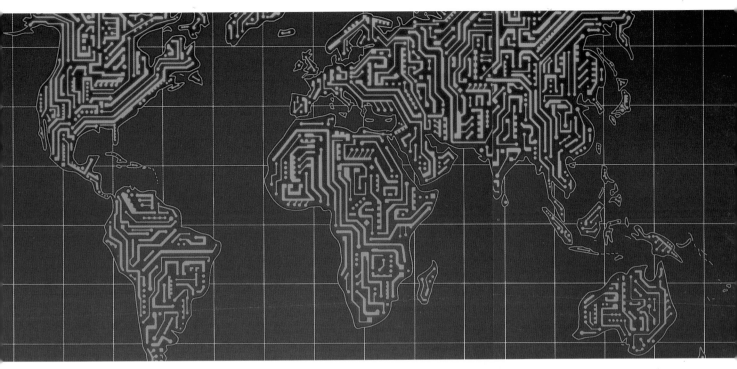

Bosch, the German automotive electronics
company, ran this image in a special
advertising insert in Fortune *(December 1986).*
The headline reads, *"Bringing microchips to
cars all over the world."*

This 1981 wine map of the world is from the
London Sunday Times *magazine. Picture and
information combine into a compelling image.*

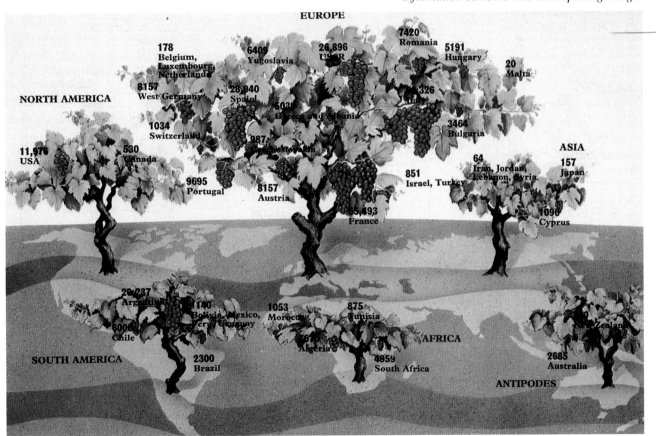

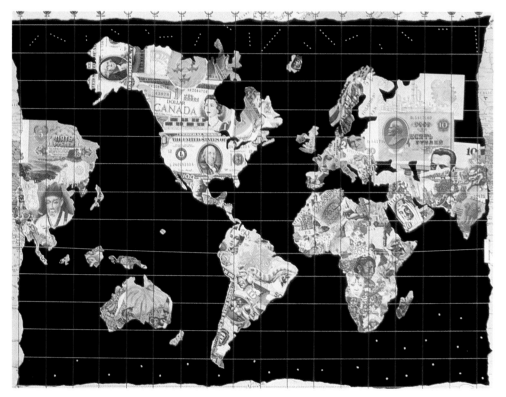

The world's money, by Lou Beach.

Europartners is a conglomerate of Italian, German, Spanish-American, and French banks with 4,600 locations around the globe. This neat arrangement of their symbol abstractly shows their sweeping coverage.

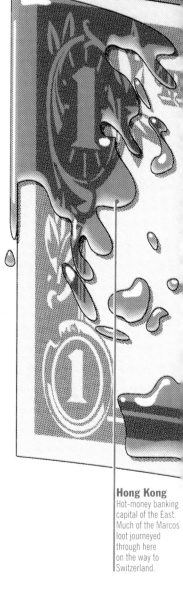

Hong Kong
Hot-money banking capital of the East. Much of the Marcos loot journeyed through here on the way to Switzerland.

In December 1989, Time *ran a cover story about the world of money laundering. Joe Lertola's inspired map (right) of dollar bills, wet with the shapes of the continents, was a great vehicle for the information about the parts of the world where transactions were made.*

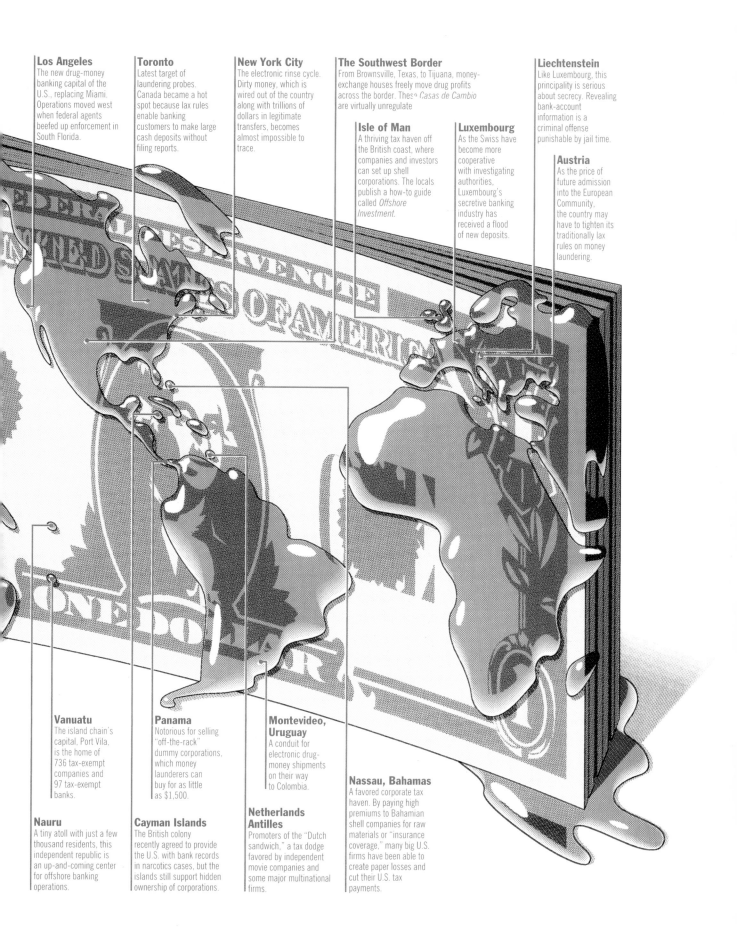

Los Angeles
The new drug-money banking capital of the U.S., replacing Miami. Operations moved west when federal agents beefed up enforcement in South Florida.

Toronto
Latest target of laundering probes. Canada became a hot spot because lax rules enable banking customers to make large cash deposits without filing reports.

New York City
The electronic rinse cycle. Dirty money, which is wired out of the country along with trillions of dollars in legitimate transfers, becomes almost impossible to trace.

The Southwest Border
From Brownsville, Texas, to Tijuana, money-exchange houses freely move drug profits across the border. These *Casas de Cambio* are virtually unregulate

Isle of Man
A thriving tax haven off the British coast, where companies and investors can set up shell corporations. The locals publish a how-to guide called *Offshore Investment.*

Luxembourg
As the Swiss have become more cooperative with investigating authorities, Luxembourg's secretive banking industry has received a flood of new deposits.

Liechtenstein
Like Luxembourg, this principality is serious about secrecy. Revealing bank-account information is a criminal offense punishable by jail time.

Austria
As the price of future admission into the European Community, the country may have to tighten its traditionally lax rules on money laundering.

Vanuatu
The island chain's capital, Port Vila, is the home of 736 tax-exempt companies and 97 tax-exempt banks.

Nauru
A tiny atoll with just a few thousand residents, this independent republic is an up-and-coming center for offshore banking operations.

Panama
Notorious for selling "off-the-rack" dummy corporations, which money launderers can buy for as little as $1,500.

Cayman Islands
The British colony recently agreed to provide the U.S. with bank records in narcotics cases, but the islands still support hidden ownership of corporations.

Montevideo, Uruguay
A conduit for electronic drug-money shipments on their way to Colombia.

Netherlands Antilles
Promoters of the "Dutch sandwich," a tax dodge favored by independent movie companies and some major multinational firms.

Nassau, Bahamas
A favored corporate tax haven. By paying high premiums to Bahamian shell companies for raw materials or "insurance coverage," many big U.S. firms have been able to create paper losses and cut their U.S. tax payments.

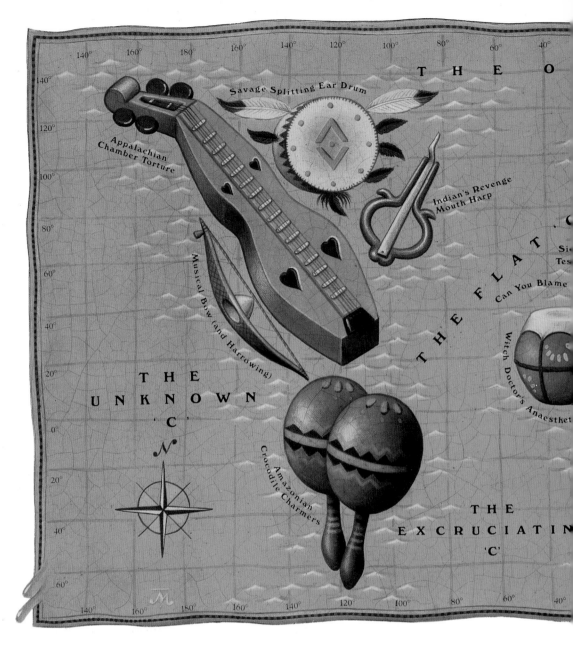

Rolling Stone's *nod to the twentieth anniversary of Earth Day, in 1990, started with this map of a polluted earth by Lane Smith. Mysterious and cryptic, the image was used on the contents page of the magazine as an overall statement about the sorry state of the world.*

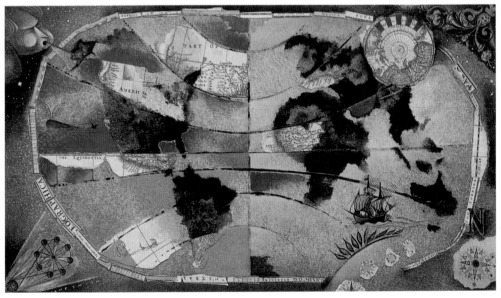

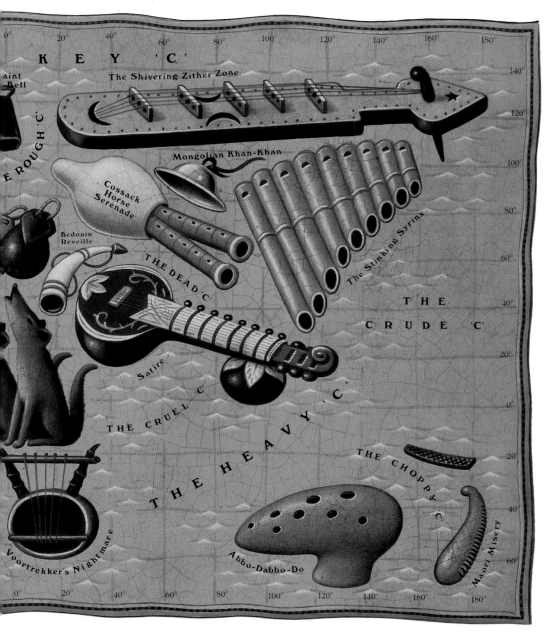

This is a wonderful painting that one would probably never guess was a map at all, if it weren't for the sea. The artist, James Marsh, has taken considerable liberties with the shapes of the real continents, but who cares? It works! The advertisement is for Yamaha's 100th anniversary, and it shows some of the musical instruments that were being played before Yamaha started making them in 1887.

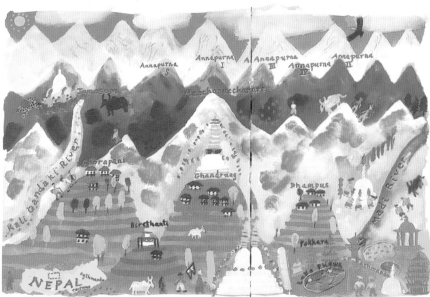

The Himalayas as interpreted by Christopher Corr for Departures magazine. The relaxed, freely painted mountains make a refreshing change from usual travel-guide maps.

An advertisement encouraging Britons to visit France via the shortest route, from Dover to Calais, uses photographic realism to help convince the reader that it is indeed a brief hop across the channel.

An advertisement for the Agusta Group, an aerospace company, lets the text do the work of outlining Italy, the company's country of operation.

Molti, pensando all'Agusta pensano subito agli elicotteri e subito dopo pensano ad elicotteri costruiti su licenza. Ciò vuol dire conoscere l'Agusta in piccola parte. Il Gruppo Agusta infatti costruisce ed esporta in tutto il mondo, non solo elicotteri, ma anche aeroplani ad ala fissa (tramite la consociata SIAI Marchetti). E oltre agli elicotteri su licenza Bell, Sikorsky e Boeing-Vertol, il Gruppo Agusta costruisce elicotteri interamente progettati in Italia, come il famoso e molto esportato A 109A. Il gruppo Agusta inquadrato nell'Efim, è costituito da 6 Società. Le Società in Italia sono: la Costruzioni Aeronautiche Giovanni Agusta di Cascina Costa; la SIAI Marchetti di Sesto Calende, Vergiate, Borgomanero e Malpensa; la Elicotteri Meridionali di Frosinone; la Industria Aeronautica Meridionale di Brindisi; le Fonderie e Officine Meccaniche di Benevento.

Nella CEE: la Agusta International di Bruxelles. Otto Stabilimenti (5 al Nord e 3 al Sud) e la notevole produzione di elicotteri ed aerei tecnologicamente all'avanguardia, fanno del Gruppo Agusta una delle più importanti imprese aerospaziali del mondo. Tutti questi fattori, insieme agli alti livelli di esportazione tanto utili alla bilancia dei pagamenti, qualificano il Gruppo Agusta come uno degli organismi più produttivi in campo nazionale. E ciò emerge chiaramente dai continui aumenti degli investimenti e dei posti di lavoro (da 2.000 a 9.000 negli ultimi dieci anni), aumenti che hanno dato un notevole contributo e impulso allo sviluppo industriale, specialmente nel Sud dell'Italia.

The cover of The Economist *(November 11, 1989) shows the future remixing of Europe, with some immediate blurring of the border between East and West Germany.*

Jean Wisenbaugh's map of the redrawn borders of Europe (below), for Business Week, *conveys the idea of being able to travel easily from Ireland right through to Greece, or up to Scandinavia, by showing a graphic wall flowing from one country to another.*

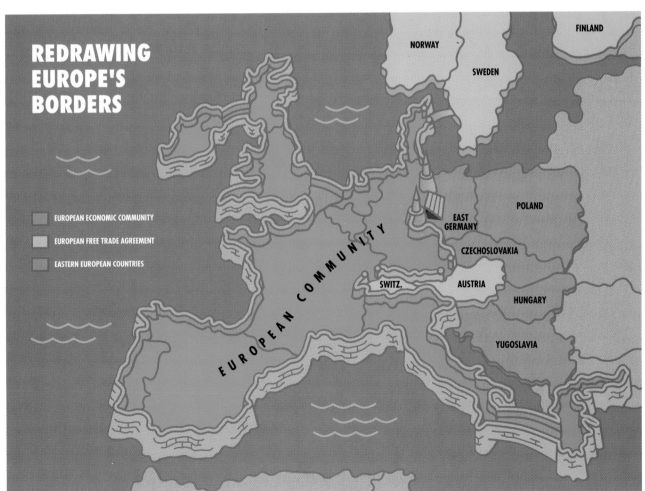

REDRAWING EUROPE'S BORDERS

- ☐ EUROPEAN ECONOMIC COMMUNITY
- ☐ EUROPEAN FREE TRADE AGREEMENT
- ☐ EASTERN EUROPEAN COUNTRIES

EUROPEAN COMMUNITY

FINLAND
NORWAY
SWEDEN
POLAND
EAST GERMANY
CZECHOSLOVAKIA
SWITZ.
AUSTRIA
HUNGARY
YUGOSLAVIA

A map of Europe by Al Lorenz, with closely
observed architectural detail sprouting up from
the landscape. A great way to show the major
tourist sights all in one view.

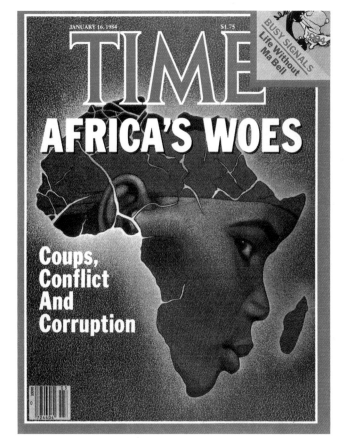

An advertisement (above) for Inter-Continental Hotels in Africa trims a photo of a lion into the shape of the continent. A simple idea, but effective.

Ronald Searle's drawing (above) of the stirrings of internal conflict in Africa appeared in Punch in 1959. While most African countries had been given their independence by 1960, the West competed with communist countries for influence there and struggled to hold onto some government control.

A panoramic view (left) of Africa, Europe, and beyond painted by Teresa Fasolino highlights just a few of the major sights in the topography, while charmingly ignoring certain geographic relationships.

This Time cover from January 1984 illustrates a story about corruption, with a face inside a continent that is beginning to crack apart. Alex Gnidziejko's realistic rendering is very powerful.

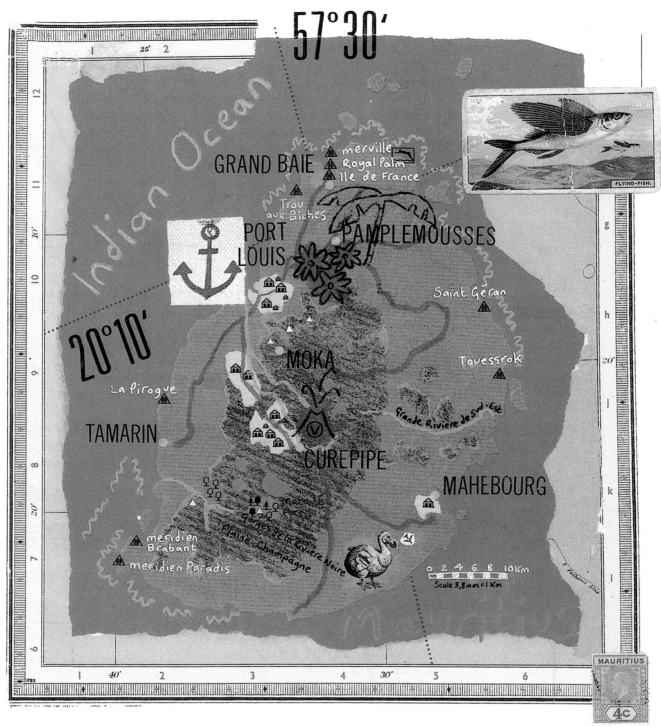

57°30'

GRAND BAIE

merville
Royal Palm
Ile de France

Trou
aux Biches

Indian Ocean

PORT LOUIS

PAMPLEMOUSSES

Saint Géran

20°10'

MOKA

Tovessrok

La Pirogue

Grande Riviere de Sud-Est

TAMARIN

CUREPIPE

MAHEBOURG

Forest
Gorges de la Riviere Noire
Plaine Champagne

meridien
Brabant

meridien Paradis

0 2 4 6 8 10Km
Scale 3,8mm=1Km

FLYING-FISH.

MAURITIUS
4c

*An unusual treatment, for a map,
at least. This image of Mauritius is
by Veronica Bailey, for the London*
Sunday Times *magazine. The loose
assemblage of collaged paper, drawn
image, and type works well and makes
you look twice.*

In 1978, twenty-five years after Mount Everest was conquered, Canada's Weekend magazine ran this map of the routes to the summit as part of a larger graphic treatment of the anniversary.

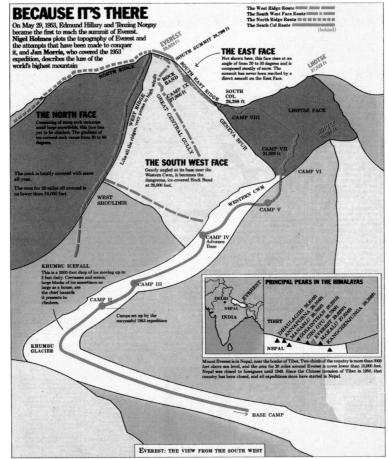

The Middle East, by Lazlo Kubinyi (below), illustrated an article in the New York Times Magazine in 1983. The artist's delicate touch is at work again here, gently delineating the region's features.

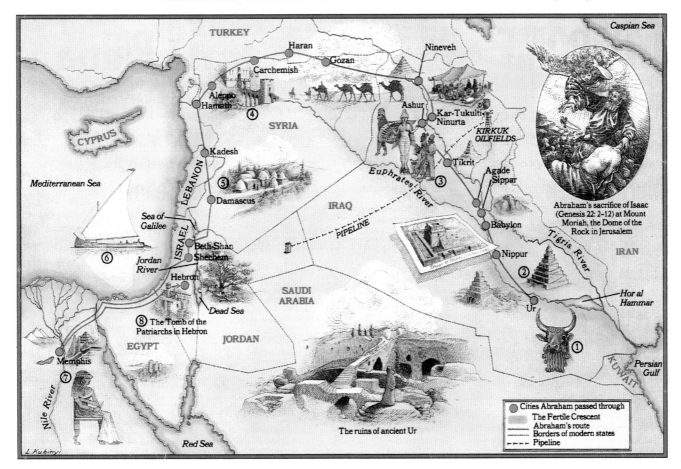

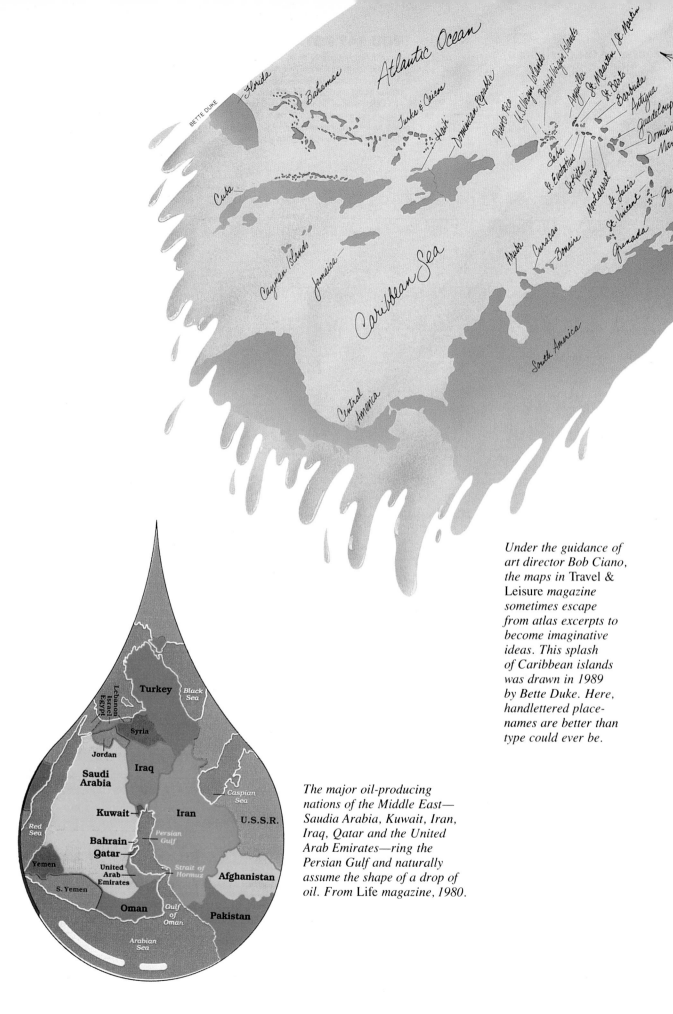

Under the guidance of
art director Bob Ciano,
the maps in Travel &
Leisure *magazine
sometimes escape
from atlas excerpts to
become imaginative
ideas. This splash
of Caribbean islands
was drawn in 1989
by Bette Duke. Here,
handlettered place-
names are better than
type could ever be.*

The major oil-producing
nations of the Middle East—
Saudia Arabia, Kuwait, Iran,
Iraq, Qatar and the United
Arab Emirates—ring the
Persian Gulf and naturally
assume the shape of a drop of
oil. From Life *magazine, 1980.*

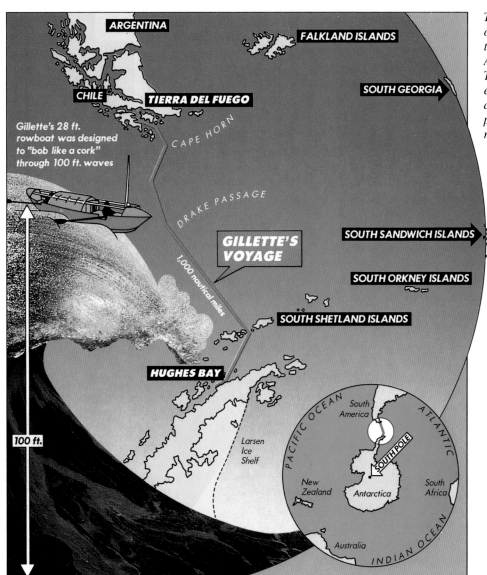

ARGENTINA

FALKLAND ISLANDS

CHILE

TIERRA DEL FUEGO

SOUTH GEORGIA

Gillette's 28 ft. rowboat was designed to "bob like a cork" through 100 ft. waves

CAPE HORN

DRAKE PASSAGE

SOUTH SANDWICH ISLANDS

GILLETTE'S VOYAGE

1,000 nautical miles

SOUTH ORKNEY ISLANDS

SOUTH SHETLAND ISLANDS

HUGHES BAY

100 ft.

Larsen Ice Shelf

PACIFIC OCEAN

South America

ATLANTIC

SOUTH POLE

New Zealand

Antarctica

South Africa

Australia

INDIAN OCEAN

This map shows the route of a rowboat voyage from the tip of South America to Antarctica, for Us magazine. The 700-foot-high waves encountered on the way are represented by a stock photography image, with the rowboat drawn to scale. The circular inset map helps the reader to understand the geography of the bottom of the world.

This map of the Hérault district of France is by David Loftus, for Departures magazine.

Nîmes

St. Guilhem-le-Désert

St. Martin-de-Londres

Montpellier

Minerve

Sète

Béziers

Narbonne

109

The technique used in Robert Lo Grippo's map of the Far East is reminiscent of nineteenth-century Chinese landscape paintings. The mountains are shown in profile, stacked on top of each other, disregarding traditional perspective.

These three plates of destinations are from a 1987 advertisement for United Airlines and American Express ("Nobody serves you the Orient like...''). These images take maps two steps away from the atlas: by aping Far Eastern scroll paintings, then by depicting them as plates. At top is a tour from Kyoto and Tokyo to Taipei and Hong Kong; center, a trip to seven Chinese cities; bottom, a historical tour of China.

An incoming Eastern Airlines jet brings drama to this beautifully painted 1987 advertising map of South America.

John Grimwade's beautifully clear graphics have graced the pages of Condé Nast Traveler magazine since its launch. In this 1991 map, he has drawn Milan's cultural monuments as simplified blocks and left the more commercial side of tourism—hotels, shopping, restaurants, and nightlife—as color-coded and numbered circles.

A detail from a bird's-eye view of Paris, drawn by Georges Peltier between 1920 and 1940. Since then several updates have taken into account the development of the city. This map was inspired by the classic view of Paris by Turgot, published in 1739.

Credited by
Departures *as an
illustration rather
than a map, this 1990
image of Cairo is by
Anthony Sidwell. Like
many of the maps in
this travel magazine,
this one departs from
being a dutiful locator
and stands as a piece
of art.*

*An advertising
postcard from
a restaurant
in Florence.*

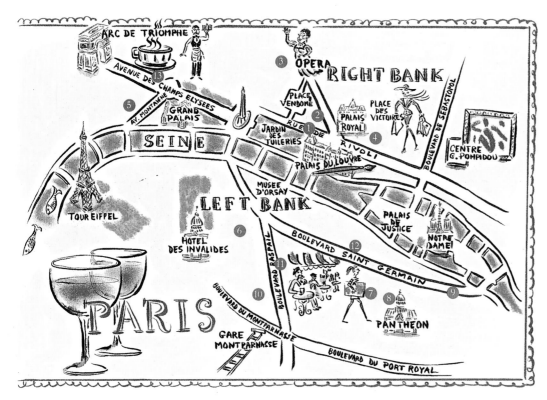

Natacha Ledwidge's delightful map of Paris, from Departures *magazine, 1990. A free, spirited illustration that locates* parfumeries *for the magazine's "secret sources" section.*

Rome (below) and its monuments, from the Civitates Orbis Terrarum *(1575). The multiple viewpoint is interesting: note the group of people standing in the foreground. Behind them the city stretches away into the distance, yet it remains flat. A few of the buildings retain the illusion of a landscape with a conventional perspective.*

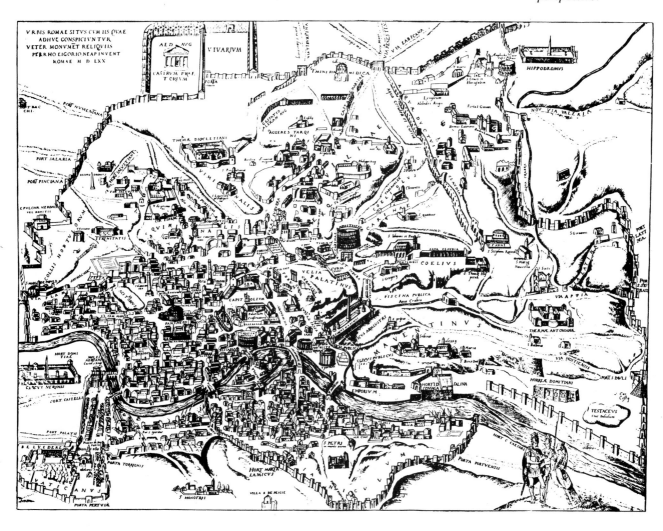

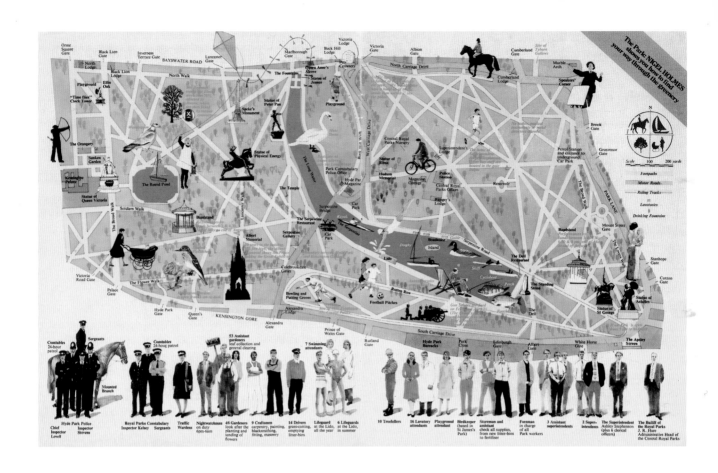

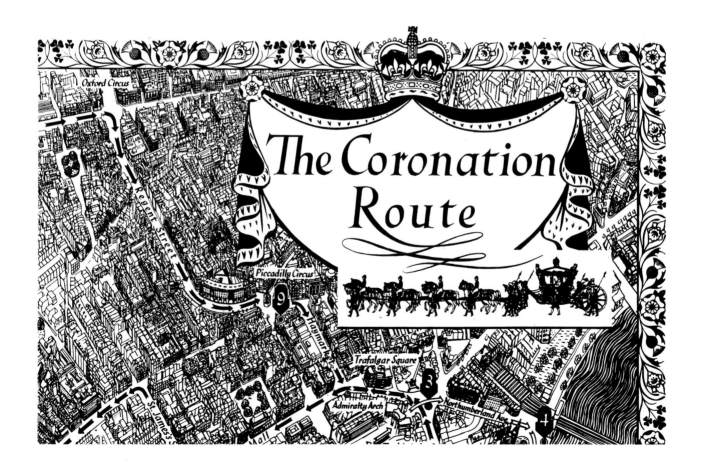

A 1977 map (left) of Hyde Park, London. Apart from including the tourist sights, the map shows the staff responsible for running the park.

Detail (below, left) from a map of Queen Elizabeth's coronation parade route, printed in Radio Times, *the BBC's weekly TV and radio magazine. The 1952 event was Britain's first major world television broadcast. Subsequently,* Radio Times *used maps and diagrams to show readers where camera and commentary positions were located. This drawing is by Cecil Bacon, a frequent contributor to the magazine between 1935 and 1968. Bacon's decorative borders and lettering were always an integral part of his maps.*

A muted drawing (right) by Ann Marshall for the Royal college of Art, London, which is the leading postgraduate art school in Britain. This elegant map shows clearly the buildings that house the various departments.

A detail (below) from John Grimwade's foldout map of the Thames River from Condé Nast Traveler *(1991). A well-organized collection of simple pictorial symbols, together with clear geographic delineation, this map invites the reader to spend time with it, and it delivers a great deal of information very elegantly.*

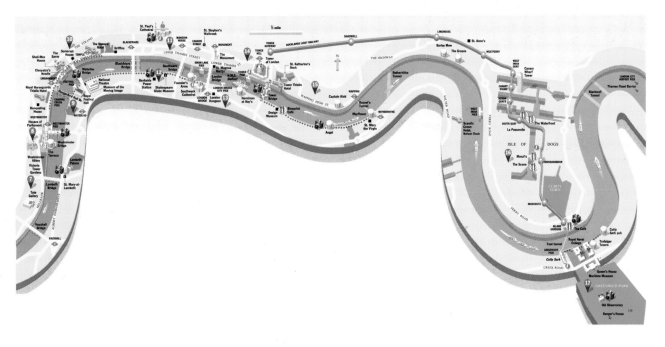

5

War, News, and the Weather

War
Elections
***USA Today*'s back page**
Satellite pictures

Hardly a week goes by at *Time* without a minor debate about whether or not to run a map of somewhere that's in the news. Do the readers know where Armenia is? Have they forgotten last week's map? Do they need a map *every* week of a continuing news story? Most people's knowledge of geography is limited, and I think it's better to err on the side of repetition than assume that everyone has a detailed mental picture of the Soviet republics, the South African homelands, or the countries of the Persian Gulf area. Many of the maps that do run in *Time* are not the pictorial sort that this book is concerned with, because the space constraints in a weekly magazine usually demand a small image. Then again, one would not want to pull out all the graphic stops *every* week.

War

During World War II, *Time*'s map room achieved an important status within the editorial division of the magazine. There was something inevitable about troop movements in a conventional war that was understood by artists drawing such maneuvers on maps. An intelligent cartographer could make as good a guess as a military analyst as to what the next move in the war might be. Looking back now at the scrap books of maps done in the early 1940s, I can appreciate the amount of work that went into thinking about the images to go with the cartographic information. Robert Chapin produced wonderfully integrated map-pictures of the war action. He was not content, even in the serious conditions of war, just to draw arrows to indicate a military push in this or that direction. He contrived to make a forceful visual equivalent to explain a strategy, while never obscuring the facts. In a map from 1944, one such ''push'' became an ''Armored Punch.'' When we moved our offices recently, I found Chapin's original pencil sketches for this map, and others. They are classical figure studies, immaculately and emotionally rendered in pencil. The maps they were part of took on a life of their own, grabbing the readers' attention and increasing their understanding of events in the war. Chapin made great play with subtle tones of gray, and he used his one available color—a bright red—to emphasize the war action that made his map important that particular week. Seeing Chapin's work in the archives of the map department when I arrived some thirty-five years later, I realized that if such a hallowed magazine could show pincers, swords, bears, flames, and blood spreading all over their maps during a war (notwithstanding the propaganda content of it), what *fun* could be had in peacetime. *Time*'s maps drawn between 1940 and 1945 thus gave me license to use unconventional imagery (primarily in charts and diagrams).

As news images, maps were regularly featured as part of the cover design of Time. *With an increasing dependence on photographic images, however, this use of pictorial maps has declined, but during war-time their use inside the magazine has been extensive.*

(Opposite page) This shows Peter Jennings, ABC television's news anchor, standing on a huge floor map used during coverage of the Persian Gulf War. Despite the January 15, 1991, deadline for the action to start, most broadcasters were ill-prepared. ABC's map was a notable exception.

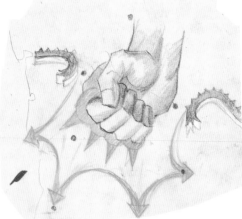

Time's *World War II cartographer Robert Chapin added meaning to maps by including visual metaphors. This map is from August 1944. Chapin's preliminary sketches show him to be part of a rare breed: an information-graphic artist who can really draw.*

In the 1980s, there were considerable changes in printing technology. The first real news opportunity to make use of these was the Falklands War. But in this case there was also a singular lack of any pictorial way to illustrate the stories other than with maps. No photographs were available: neither side would release any pictures of the action. *Time* kept a chartered plane at the ready in Buenos Aires for the duration of the war, waiting for clearance to take photographers and reporters to the islands. It was particularly ironic that they never got there, since the technological advances that were enabling newspapers and magazines to print entirely in color had led them to trumpet their intention to use more and larger pictures. Editors, desperate for images to fill pages that had been so extensively advertised as being a viable competitor with television, started to talk about the importance of information graphics. That hard-won quota of color pages had to be filled somehow. So with the Falklands War, a new generation of map and graphic artists around the world suddenly grew up.

Not that graphic reporting of war was new. The *Illustrated London News* had printed artists' impressions of the two world wars and the Boer War before that; back, in fact, to the American Civil War. In those days, on-the-spot sketches were sent to London, where they were physically cut up and divided among several wood engravers, each of whom worked on their own separate part of the whole image. The resulting engraved wood-blocks were then bolted together to produce a printable reproduction of the complete original drawing. About 1880, photoengraving, which could directly reproduce the original drawing, cut out the need for such a laborious production method.

Some of the maps of the Falklands War, and subsequently of the actions in Grenada and Panama, suffered from stretching too little information too far. This was the direct result of wanting to fill up spaces that would normally have been occupied by photographs. Information artists rushed to their copies of *Jane's All the World's Aircraft, Ships and Weapons Systems* the moment a military briefing indicated what hardware had been used in an engagement. They then all too readily fixed on a view of a fighter-bomber swooping into the page, the map, and the war zone, for the kill. Arrows became three-dimensional, often indicating with too much graphic passion the landing of an aircraft, or worse, just pointing to something on the map. A bold arrow like that should only be used when there is *movement* to be shown, never as a pointer joining a remote block of type to something drawn on the map.

During the long buildup to the 1991 Persian Gulf War, every graphic trick in the book was used to explain the possible course that the war might take. Large, elegantly curving red arrows were used indiscriminately, and it often looked as though the war had already broken out. When it did, there was so little information available that the media struggled to find new angles. Military censorship on the ground in Saudi Arabia and Israel, not to mention *disinformation* from Iraq, prevented the world from getting much detail, but that didn't stop the speculation in pictures and words about how the war was proceeding or what might happen next. The nonstop coverage on television, most notably CNN, made little use of good maps, despite having had five months in which to prepare them. Included in that time was the United Nation's decision to impose a deadline for Iraqi withdrawal from Kuwait. After that deadline, the Allied armies were allowed to use force, and probably would. When the Super Bowl or an election is covered by television or the press, there are plenty of prepared graphics waiting to be filled in as the actions and results are announced. Maybe we all just hoped that the Gulf War would never happen.

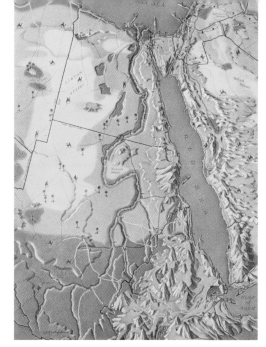

Today, news magazines and broadcasting companies regularly spin off collections of their work on world events into books. Time *did this during World War II with maps of different theaters of action. Above is a detail from North Africa, by Ernest Baker, and below, Southern England and the coast of France, by Aldren Watson, from* Time, *July 22, 1940, the eve of Hitler's air attack on England.*

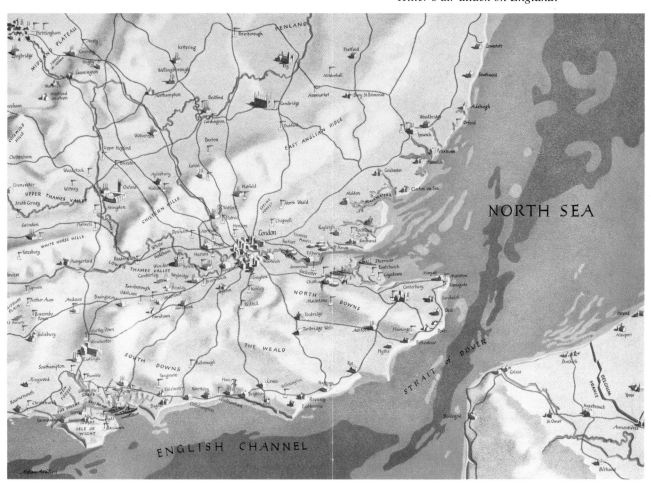

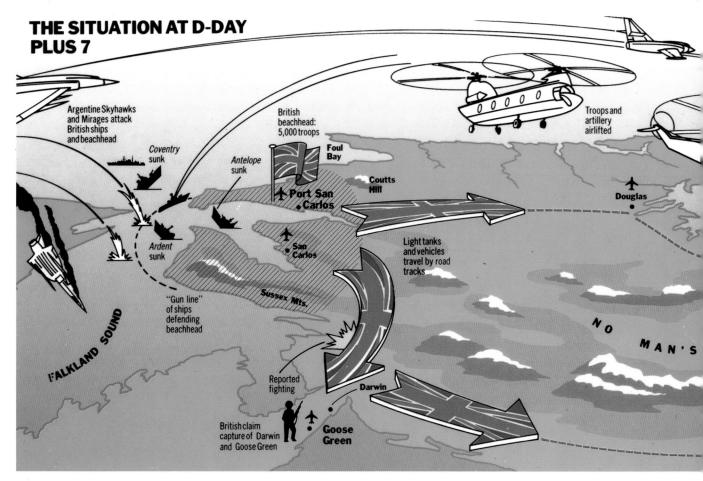

THE SITUATION AT D-DAY PLUS 7

Argentine Skyhawks and Mirages attack British ships and beachhead

Coventry sunk

Antelope sunk

British beachhead: 5,000 troops

Foul Bay

Coutts Hill

Port San Carlos

San Carlos

Ardent sunk

"Gun line" of ships defending beachhead

FALKLAND SOUND

Sussex Mts.

Reported fighting

British claim capture of Darwin and Goose Green

Darwin

Goose Green

Light tanks and vehicles travel by road tracks

Troops and artillery airlifted

Douglas

NO MAN'S

During the Falklands War, Time *used new printing technology to make last-minute changes to battle maps. In 1982, computers were not generally used for drawing images of this sort. But airplanes, arrows, and land-shapes drawn by hand could be scanned, combined and colored on a computer, and the output from that process became the artwork. So instead of laboriously pasting-up type, drawings, and map bases at the drawing board, the process was done electronically— albeit remote from the designer's office. In the few years since the Falklands War, computers have come down in size and price and reside on the desk of most magazine and newspaper mapmakers, replacing their drawing boards completely.*

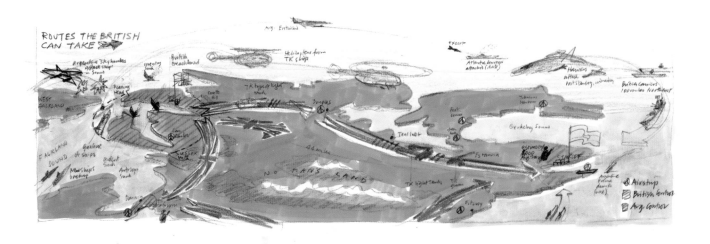

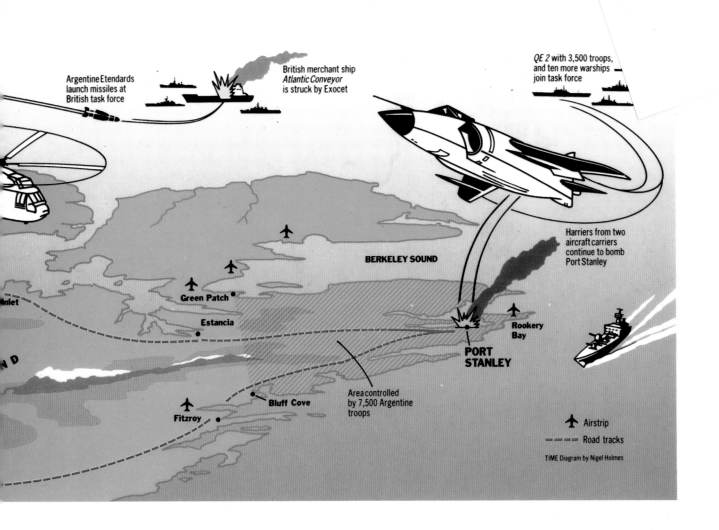

Argentine Etendards
launch missiles at
British task force

British merchant ship
Atlantic Conveyor
is struck by Exocet

QE 2 with 3,500 troops,
and ten more warships
join task force

BERKELEY SOUND

Green Patch

Estancia

Harriers from two
aircraft carriers
continue to bomb
Port Stanley

Rookery
Bay

**PORT
STANLEY**

Area controlled
by 7,500 Argentine
troops

Bluff Cove

Fitzroy

Inlet

✈ Airstrip

- - - Road tracks

TIME Diagram by Nigel Holmes

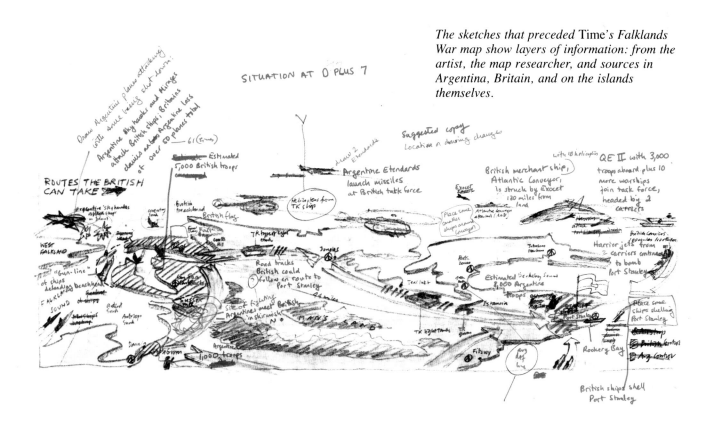

The sketches that preceded Time's Falklands
War map show layers of information: from the
artist, the map researcher, and sources in
Argentina, Britain, and on the islands
themselves.

SITUATION AT O PLUS 7

ROUTES THE BRITISH
CAN TAKE?

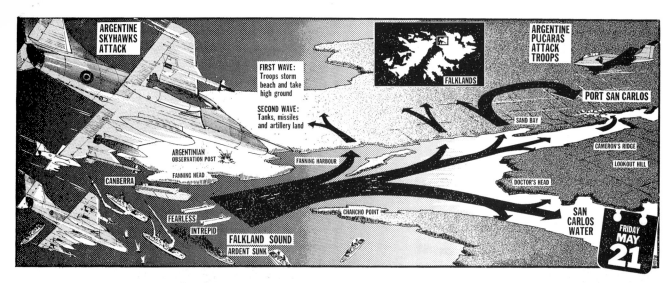

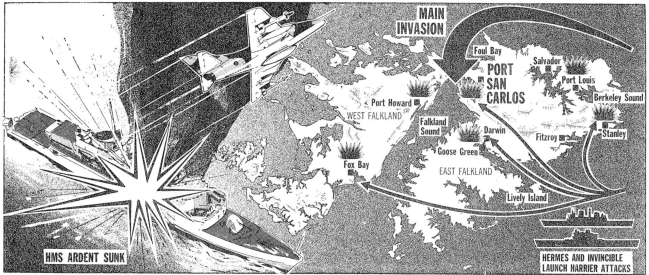

(Top) The Falklands, by Phil Green,
for the London Sunday Times.

(Center) The Falklands,
from the London Sunday Times,
May 23, 1982, by Gordon Beckett.

(Right) The Falklands,
from the Chicago Tribune.

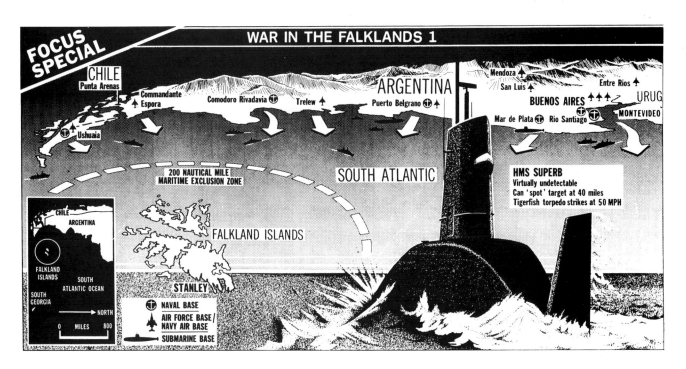

FOCUS SPECIAL

CHILE — **Punta Arenas**

Commandante Espora · **Comodoro Rivadavia** · **Trelew** · **Puerto Belgrano**

ARGENTINA

Mendoza · San Luis · Entre Rios

BUENOS AIRES — URUG

Mar de Plata · Rio Santiago — MONTEVIDEO

Ushuaia

200 NAUTICAL MILE MARITIME EXCLUSION ZONE

SOUTH ATLANTIC

FALKLAND ISLANDS

HMS SUPERB
Virtually undetectable
Can 'spot' target at 40 miles
Tigerfish torpedo strikes at 50 MPH

STANLEY

CHILE / ARGENTINA

FALKLAND ISLANDS

SOUTH ATLANTIC OCEAN

SOUTH GEORGIA

→ NORTH

0 — MILES — 800

🛲 NAVAL BASE
✈ AIR FORCE BASE / NAVY AIR BASE
🛥 SUBMARINE BASE

War and Peace at a Glance: Major Military and Diplomatic Actions in the Falklands

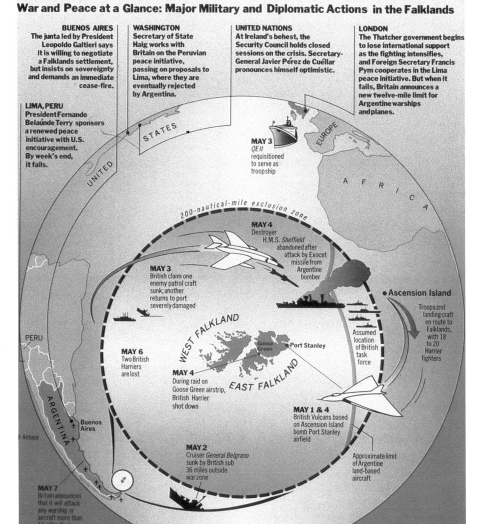

BUENOS AIRES
The junta led by President Leopoldo Galtieri says it is willing to negotiate a Falklands settlement, but insists on sovereignty and demands an immediate cease-fire.

WASHINGTON
Secretary of State Haig works with Britain on the Peruvian peace initiative, passing on proposals to Lima, where they are eventually rejected by Argentina.

UNITED NATIONS
At Ireland's behest, the Security Council holds closed sessions on the crisis. Secretary-General Javier Pérez de Cuéllar pronounces himself optimistic.

LONDON
The Thatcher government begins to lose international support as the fighting intensifies, and Foreign Secretary Francis Pym cooperates in the Lima peace initiative. But when it fails, Britain announces a new twelve-mile limit for Argentine warships and planes.

LIMA, PERU
President Fernando Belaúnde Terry sponsors a renewed peace initiative with U.S. encouragement. By week's end, it fails.

MAY 3 QE II requisitioned to serve as troop ship

200-nautical-mile exclusion zone

MAY 4 Destroyer H.M.S. *Sheffield* abandoned after attack by Exocet missile from Argentine bomber

MAY 3 British claim one enemy patrol craft sunk; another returns to port severely damaged

MAY 6 Two British Harriers are lost

MAY 4 During raid on Goose Green airstrip, British Harrier shot down

WEST FALKLAND · Goose Green · Port Stanley · EAST FALKLAND

Assumed location of British task force

● Ascension Island
Troops and landing craft en route to Falklands, with 18 to 20 Harrier fighters

MAY 1 & 4 British Vulcans based on Ascension Island bomb Port Stanley airfield

MAY 2 Cruiser *General Belgrano* sunk by British sub 36 miles outside war zone

Approximate limit of Argentine land-based aircraft

PERU · ARGENTINA · Buenos Aires · Airbase

MAY 7 Britain announces that it will attack any warship or aircraft more than 12 miles from Argentine coast

UNITED STATES · EUROPE · AFRICA

(Above) The Falklands, from the London Sunday Times, *May 23, 1982.*

Photographs of the action in the Falklands were so hard to come by that maps were expected to fill the void in magazines and newspapers, as readers had come to expect war stories to be illustrated. This map from Time *detailed the diplomatic activity in cities on both sides of the Atlantic and took a close-up look at the week's maneuvers around the Falkland Islands themselves.*

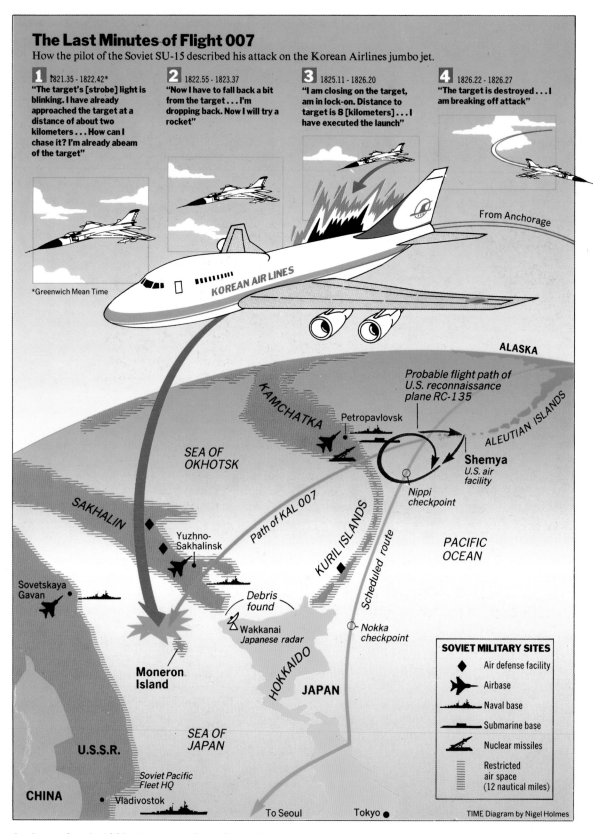

The Last Minutes of Flight 007

How the pilot of the Soviet SU-15 described his attack on the Korean Airlines jumbo jet.

1 1821.35 - 1822.42*
"The target's [strobe] light is blinking. I have already approached the target at a distance of about two kilometers . . . How can I chase it? I'm already abeam of the target"

*Greenwich Mean Time

2 1822.55 - 1823.37
"Now I have to fall back a bit from the target . . . I'm dropping back. Now I will try a rocket"

3 1825.11 - 1826.20
"I am closing on the target, am in lock-on. Distance to target is 8 [kilometers] . . . I have executed the launch"

4 1826.22 - 1826.27
"The target is destroyed . . . I am breaking off attack"

KOREAN AIR LINES

From Anchorage

ALASKA

Probable flight path of U.S. reconnaissance plane RC-135

KAMCHATKA

Petropavlovsk

ALEUTIAN ISLANDS

Shemya
U.S. air facility

SEA OF OKHOTSK

Nippi checkpoint

SAKHALIN

Path of KAL 007

KURIL ISLANDS

PACIFIC OCEAN

Yuzhno-Sakhalinsk

Scheduled route

Sovetskaya Gavan

Debris found

Wakkanai
Japanese radar

Nokka checkpoint

Moneron Island

HOKKAIDO

JAPAN

SOVIET MILITARY SITES

◆ Air defense facility

✈ Airbase

— Naval base

— Submarine base

Nuclear missiles

Restricted air space (12 nautical miles)

SEA OF JAPAN

U.S.S.R.

Soviet Pacific Fleet HQ

CHINA

• Vladivostok

To Seoul   Tokyo •

TIME Diagram by Nigel Holmes

On September 1, 1983, Korean Airlines flight 007 was shot down off the coast of Hokkaido by a Soviet SU-15 fighter, killing all 269 passengers aboard. The Russians claimed it was a spy plane. The route and details of the encounter are shown in this diagram, which combines the action in the sky with the geography of the area below. It was later proved that the KAL flight had strayed much further off course than this map shows.

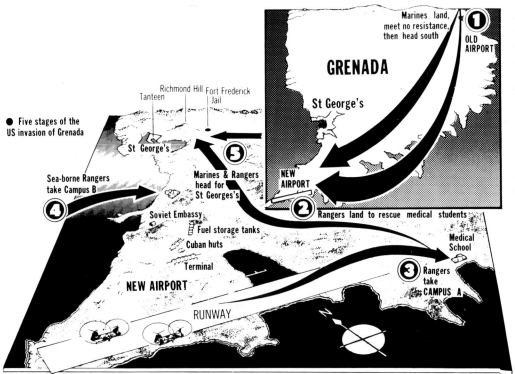

Peter Sullivan's maps and diagrams for the London Sunday Times *set a standard for newspaper graphics around the world. His technique of incorporating dramatic illustrations into the information has been widely imitated. Here, his map of the invasion of Grenada in 1983.*

In the map (img_2) the following labels appear:

Marines land, meet no resistance, then head south

GRENADA

OLD AIRPORT

St George's

NEW AIRPORT

①

Richmond Hill
Tanteen | Fort Frederick Jail

St George's

● Five stages of the US invasion of Grenada

⑤

④ Sea-borne Rangers take Campus B

Marines & Rangers head for St George's

② Rangers land to rescue medical students

Soviet Embassy

Fuel storage tanks

Cuban huts

Terminal

NEW AIRPORT

Medical School

③ Rangers take CAMPUS A

RUNWAY

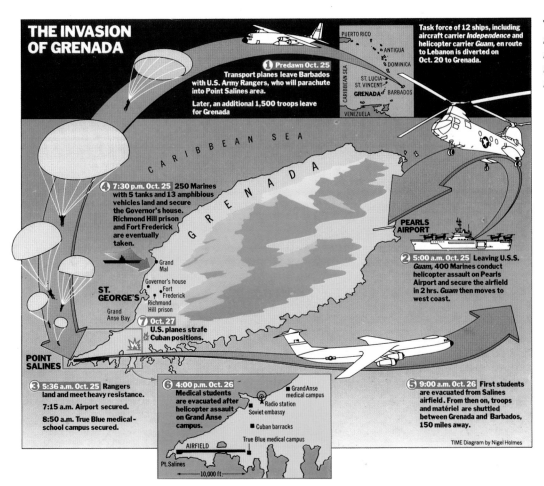

Time's Grenada map simplified the topography of the island and dramatized the air invasion.

THE INVASION OF GRENADA

① **Predawn Oct. 25** Transport planes leave Barbados with U.S. Army Rangers, who will parachute into Point Salines area.

Later, an additional 1,500 troops leave for Grenada

PUERTO RICO
ANTIGUA
DOMINICA
CARIBBEAN SEA
ST. LUCIA
ST. VINCENT
GRENADA
BARBADOS
VENEZUELA

Task force of 12 ships, including aircraft carrier *Independence* and helicopter carrier *Guam,* en route to Lebanon is diverted on Oct. 20 to Grenada.

CARIBBEAN SEA

GRENADA

④ **7:30 p.m. Oct. 25** 250 Marines with 5 tanks and 13 amphibious vehicles land and secure the Governor's house. Richmond Hill prison and Fort Frederick are eventually taken.

PEARLS AIRPORT

② **5:00 a.m. Oct. 25** Leaving U.S.S. *Guam,* 400 Marines conduct helicopter assault on Pearls Airport and secure the airfield in 2 hrs. *Guam* then moves to west coast.

Grand Mal

Governor's house

Fort Frederick

Richmond Hill prison

ST. GEORGE'S

Grand Anse Bay

⑦ **Oct. 27** U.S. planes strafe Cuban positions.

POINT SALINES

③ **5:36 a.m. Oct. 25** Rangers land and meet heavy resistance.

7:15 a.m. Airport secured.

8:50 a.m. True Blue medical-school campus secured.

⑥ **4:00 p.m. Oct. 26** Medical students are evacuated after helicopter assault on Grand Anse campus.

Grand Anse medical campus

Radio station

Soviet embassy

Cuban barracks

True Blue medical campus

AIRFIELD

Pt. Salines

10,000 ft.

⑤ **9:00 a.m. Oct. 26** First students are evacuated from Salines airfield. From then on, troops and matériel are shuttled between Grenada and Barbados, 150 miles away.

TIME Diagram by Nigel Holmes

In the months leading up to the outbreak of fighting in the Persian Gulf War, the media tried to find different angles on the situation in Iraq. This Time map from September 1990 shows the four main groups of targets to be attacked by allied forces.

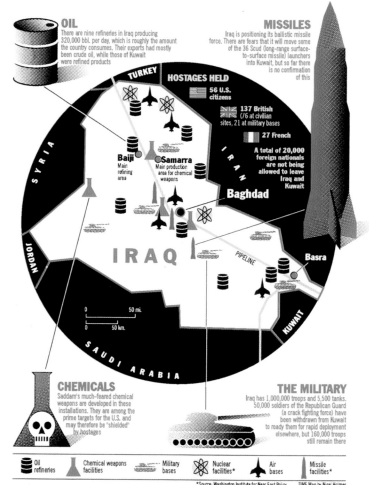

Having practiced their maps in print for five months, magazines and newspapers seemed better prepared than the broadcast media when the Persian Gulf War actually started in January 1991. This splendid map from the French magazine Le Nouvel Observateur shows a sophisticated treatment of the action in the sky.

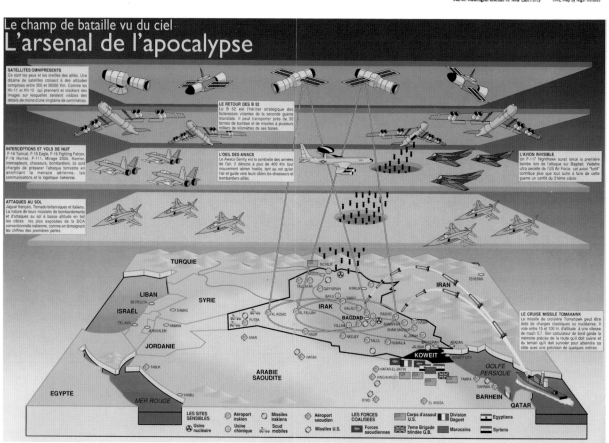

News

Election coverage can really benefit from pictorial help. The system of electing officials in the United States is such a long process that we all tire of it before the campaign is half over. Two examples shown here add a sense of humor to the statistics of the final outcome (both a Republican and a Democratic victory were prepared, in case of an upset at the last moment).

How much license is permitted when preparing maps of an election victory? Does it trivialize the information when maps look like elephants or donkeys? The answer about when to draw the line is simple: the reason for the map is to inform. If you cannot read the information, the map has failed. If, in a magazine or newspaper that has been full of election maps for almost two years, you would like to amuse *as well as* inform, then so much the better. Boring maps of mandatory information are a sin. You might as well ignore the mandate to print an election-results map if readers are not going to look at it.

There are two sides in the debate about graphic enhancement of information. The academic side takes the view that information is intrinsically interesting and should on no account be decorated, dressed up, or otherwise be made easy or exciting to look at. This view optimistically contends that all readers are (*a*) intelligent, (*b*) have a lot of time on their hands for the express purpose of reading maps put out by the popular press, and (*c*) are desperately interested in the subject matter and need no encouragement to read it. On the other side, many in the news business question the academic conclusions. I *do* believe that readers *are* intelligent, and it is not patronizing to give them a picture to look at, it is friendly—*user-friendly,* to borrow the computer catchphrase. Also, I know that readers don't have a lot of time to spend reading, or perhaps I should say they do not spend a lot of their time reading. That's why they pick up magazines in the first place: They want a summary, and they want it fast. If the point of a graphic does not come across quickly they'll move on. They will also move on if the point is hidden under too much picture, so some restraints are necessary to ensure that the message is understood. I do not advocate flippant decoration, especially when the intent of a graphic is serious. Whenever embellishment gets in the way, it's wrong. So both sides have a point. True, there are joys in being confronted with pure information and having the time to ponder and interpret it. But editing is not new; editing so that readers can get the meaning more quickly, editing to bring out a certain point more strongly than others, editing to help understanding, editing with wit.

I'm purposely discussing this question in the chapter on news maps, since news maps have the greatest potential to describe

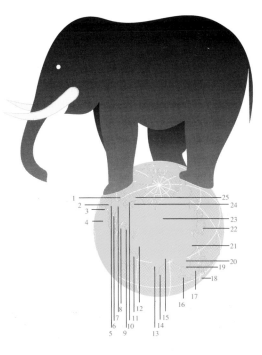

Every information graphics designer should ask this question: Have I overpowered the information *with my* illustration? *If the information on a map is rendered unintelligible in order to make way for a picture, you've gone too far toward illustration. Grabbing readers' attention is fine, but if they can't read the type, why get their attention?*

serious matters. A war is serious—but can we not show aircraft and tanks in combat? Indira Ghandi is shot—but can the graphic artist not use all the available research to reconstruct the action, drawing it so that readers get a clear impression of the location and the sequence of events? This is not trivialization, it is teaching through demonstration, through metaphor, through symbolism. Call it overdecorated chart-junk if you will, but watch your readers disappear as you preach from an ivory tower.

Sketches for a Bush election victory try ways to combine the elephant with the map.

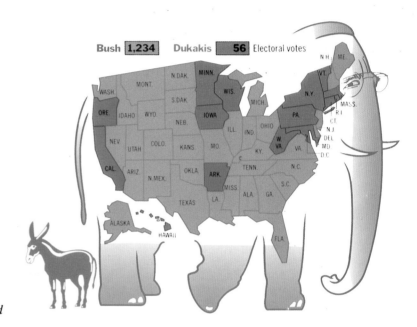

There have been famous upsets in the conventional wisdom about who'll win a presidential election (though not recently), and the print media must be prepared for that and be able to switch to plan B at short notice, if they are going to appear on the newsstands as soon as they'd like to in this competitive age. Thus Time *always makes two versions of its election packages, just in case. For the 1988 election, these simple maps of the states were dressed in Thomas Nast's symbolic elephant and donkey outfits, their faces simple caricatures of Bush and Dukakis.*

Sketch preceding the Democratic map.

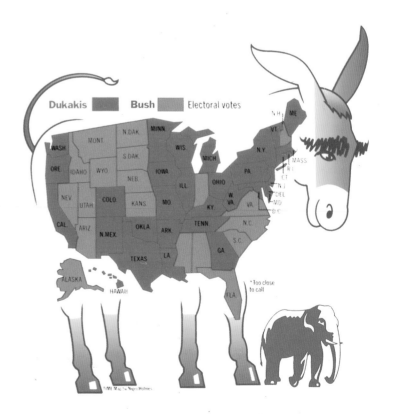

INDIRA'S LAST WALK

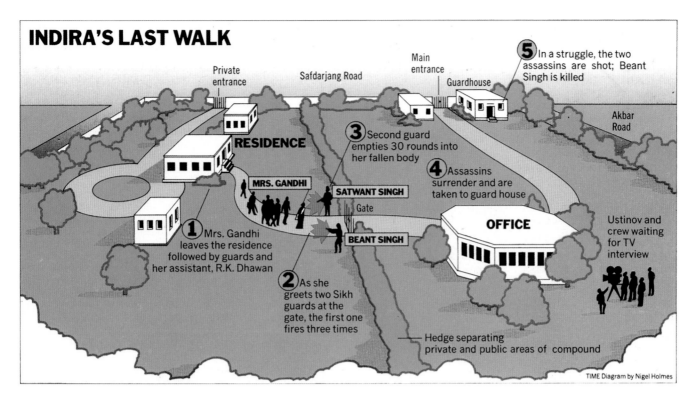

Private entrance

Safdarjang Road

Main entrance

Guardhouse

5 In a struggle, the two assassins are shot; Beant Singh is killed

Akbar Road

RESIDENCE

3 Second guard empties 30 rounds into her fallen body

4 Assassins surrender and are taken to guard house

MRS. GANDHI

SATWANT SINGH

Gate

1 Mrs. Gandhi leaves the residence followed by guards and her assistant, R.K. Dhawan

BEANT SINGH

OFFICE

Ustinov and crew waiting for TV interview

2 As she greets two Sikh guards at the gate, the first one fires three times

Hedge separating private and public areas of compound

TIME Diagram by Nigel Holmes

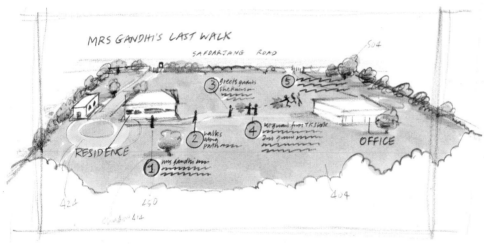

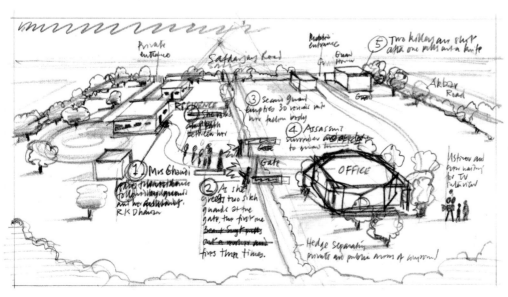

Time's map of Indira Gandhi's last walk illustrates an article about the Indian prime minister's shooting in 1984. With press deadlines approaching, this map was constructed from information received in telephone conversations with colleagues in England who had visited the location of the assassination. This rough color sketch was the first attempt to visualize the action. The second sketch concentrated on the details of the assassination and began to pin down the final text.

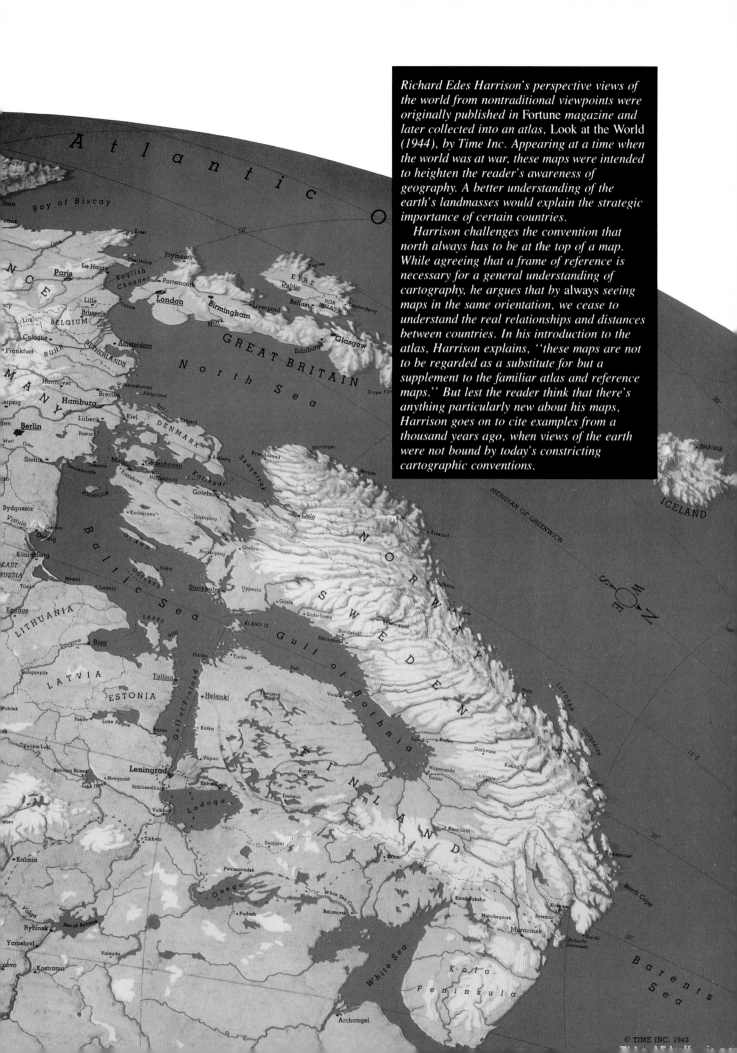

Richard Edes Harrison's perspective views of the world from nontraditional viewpoints were originally published in Fortune *magazine and later collected into an atlas,* Look at the World *(1944), by Time Inc. Appearing at a time when the world was at war, these maps were intended to heighten the reader's awareness of geography. A better understanding of the earth's landmasses would explain the strategic importance of certain countries.*

Harrison challenges the convention that north always has to be at the top of a map. While agreeing that a frame of reference is necessary for a general understanding of cartography, he argues that by always seeing maps in the same orientation, we cease to understand the real relationships and distances between countries. In his introduction to the atlas, Harrison explains, ''these maps are not to be regarded as a substitute for but a supplement to the familiar atlas and reference maps.'' But lest the reader think that there's anything particularly new about his maps, Harrison goes on to cite examples from a thousand years ago, when views of the earth were not bound by today's constricting cartographic conventions.

When USA Today was launched in 1982, one of its most dramatic features was the back page, devoted entirely to the nation's weather. (It has since sold a strip of space at the bottom to advertisers). The designer was George Rorick, who not only developed the paper's concept of the daily color map, and the attendant graphic that examines one aspect of the weather in detail, but also worked out the complicated technical details of getting it all onto the paper's satellite network and into print every day.

WEATHER ACROSS THE USA

Pacific Coast: Partly to mostly cloudy in Washington and Oregon with scattered showers and some mountain snow. Intervals of clouds and sunshine in Northern California, sunny in Southern California.

Rockies: Morning snow flurries in east-central sections. Some rain and mountain snow showers across the far north. Mostly sunny in the southwest, partly cloudy elsewhere.

South Central: Snow, sleet and freezing rain in northeast Kansas and northwest Missouri. Showers and rain in Oklahoma and the rest of Missouri, thunderstorms from eastern Texas to Arkansas and Louisiana.

North Central: Snow and sleet spreading from Nebraska and western Iowa into eastern Iowa and extreme southern Minnesota. Freezing rain in southeastern Iowa. Partly to mostly cloudy in the north.

Midwest: Rain spreading from the west into Illinois, southern and western Indiana and western Kentucky. Snow and ice possible in extreme northwestern Illinois and southwestern Wisconsin by late afternoon.

Southeast: Mostly sunny in Florida, a few afternoon thunderstorms possible. Partly to mostly cloudy and cool in the northeast. Showers and thunderstorms, perhaps heavy, moving into the west.

Northeast: Variable amount of cloudiness, including sunshine in a few spots. More sunshine in eastern New England, elsewhere nothing more than a bit of drizzle or a few flurries.

FOUR-DAY HIGHLIGHTS

c (cloudy); i (ice); pc (partly cloudy); r (rain); s (sunny); sf (snow flurries); sh (showers); sn (snow)

State	City	Yest'day	Today	Tues.	Wed.
Alabama	Birmingham	82/47pc	76/52pc	85/44sh	65/46pc
	Mobile	74/56c	78/57pc	70/53sh	72/52pc
Alaska	Anchorage	33/24s	40/27pc	40/27pc	42/27c
	Fairbanks	13/-2s	35/8s	38/10s	40/12s
Arizona	Flagstaff	54/23s	57/25s	60/28s	60/30pc
	Phoenix	75/50s	80/53s	82/55s	82/55s
Arkansas	Ft. Smith	55/52sh	56/43sh	49/42c	52/42pc
	Little Rock	56/52c	58/45sh	50/43c	53/43pc
Calif.	Los Angeles	76/58pc	76/52s	74/52s	72/52pc
	Sacramento	66/42pc	74/50pc	72/50c	69/48pc
	San Diego	76/55pc	77/57s	77/57s	74/55s
	San Francisco	66/55pc	64/52pc	62/49pc	59/46pc
	San Jose	68/46pc	67/45pc	65/42pc	63/40pc
Colorado	Aspen	36/30sn	37/15sf	27/18sf	37/20sn
	Denver	39/28sn	43/30pc	53/33s	50/35c
Conn.	Hartford	37/22c	41/35r	48/34c	49/38r
Delaware	Wilmington	48/38c	49/38c	56/42c	50/38r
D.C.	Washington	57/42c	53/42c	58/45c	52/40r
Florida	Jacksonville	81/55s	80/57s	77/59sh	76/55pc
	Miami	82/59s	82/64s	82/66s	80/64pc
	Orlando	83/59s	81/58s	79/60sh	77/57pc
	Tampa	82/56s	82/62s	82/60pc	78/59sh
Georgia	Atlanta	76/54pc	73/56pc	76/56r	68/45sh
	Columbus	84/56s	75/58pc	76/57r	69/48sh
Hawaii	Hilo	82/67sh	82/63s	82/63s	82/63s
	Honolulu	82/65s	85/66s	85/65s	85/65s
Idaho	Boise	48/27c	52/40pc	53/27sh	48/34sh
	Pocatello	40/26pc	48/37pc	48/35sh	46/34sh
Illinois	Chicago	30/27sn	39/33r	45/36r	43/35c
	Peoria	32/28c	43/35r	48/39r	46/30c
Indiana	Ft. Wayne	31/25i	43/35c	50/43r	46/37c
	Indianapolis	34/30sn	50/45c	58/47r	50/30c
Iowa	Davenport	33/28c	40/35i	38/32c	44/30pc
	Des Moines	32/26c	36/33i	35/27sf	42/29pc
Kansas	Topeka	35/32i	37/32sn	43/29c	52/32pc
	Wichita	40/34r	43/36sh	50/36pc	58/39pc
Kentucky	Lexington	46/35c	57/49c	59/50r	53/40c
	Louisville	49/39c	58/50c	60/50r	54/41c
La.	New Orleans	76/53c	75/52r	64/50pc	68/53pc
	Shreveport	80/64c	64/44pc	55/41c	60/42pc
Maine	Bangor	31/28c	33/32i	37/34r	41/32c
	Portland	30/26i	35/34r	39/35r	44/34c
Md.	Baltimore	49/38c	52/38c	57/43c	50/38r
	Cumberland	53/43c	51/38c	59/44c	51/39sh
Mass.	Boston	30/28i	36/34r	40/36r	45/36c
	Springfield	37/34r	41/35r	47/35c	
Michigan	Detroit	32/25sn	39/32c	48/40sh	45/35sh
	Marquette	25/12sn	27/22pc	31/25c	33/22sn
Minn.	Duluth	27/10pc	30/17pc	30/19pc	32/22c
	Mpls.-St. Paul	32/16pc	39/25pc	39/27pc	38/24c
Miss.	Jackson	81/59c	74/49sh	60/44c	62/46pc
	Tupelo	78/57c	72/46sh	58/43c	59/44pc
Missouri	Kansas City	35/30c	38/32r	38/30c	47/31pc
	St. Louis	39/33c	45/34r	51/32r	50/32pc
Mont.	Billings	51/35pc	58/36sh	58/36c	49/31sf
	Great Falls	51/29pc	55/32sh	55/32c	45/27sf
Nebraska	Grand Island	30/27sn	36/29sn	40/29sf	44/27c
	Omaha	29/26c	36/31sn	39/28sf	39/28pc
Nevada	Las Vegas	64/47pc	74/50s	77/52pc	72/48pc
	Reno	56/26pc	46/33c	46/33sh	44/29c
N.H.	Berlin	33/29c	31/29i	33/32r	41/33c
	Concord	35/31c	33/31i	36/33r	43/32c
N.J.	Atlantic City	45/36c	47/37c	53/39c	48/39r
	Newark	47/34c	44/35c	48/38c	50/38r
N.M.	Albuquerque	58/30pc	59/32pc	63/34s	66/34pc
	Roswell	65/44s	65/44pc	68/47s	70/47pc
N.Y.	Albany	37/24c	35/33r	42/30c	46/34c
	Buffalo	33/20c	35/27c	46/30c	43/34r
	New York	43/31c	44/37r	48/35c	50/38r
N.C.	Asheville	58/42c	63/48pc	72/56pc	50/44sh
	Charlotte	61/50c	64/49pc	73/58pc	60/46sh
N.D.	Bismarck	31/22c	42/26pc	42/28c	40/26c
	Fargo	34/20c	42/26pc	42/26c	40/26c
Ohio	Cincinnati	38/33c	53/45c	59/48r	50/40c
	Cleveland	30/23i	44/34c	53/40c	43/36c
Okla.	Oklahoma City	66/45r	43/34r	45/32c	54/36pc
	Tulsa	57/45sh	46/36r	45/33c	52/35pc
Oregon	Bend	51/32c	50/33c	50/35sh	47/30pc
	Portland	53/45c	62/44c	60/44r	56/42pc
Pa.	Philadelphia	44/36c	49/37c	55/46c	52/40sh
	Pittsburgh	43/32c	50/38c	60/44c	52/40sh
	Wilkes-Barre	43/26c	40/32pc	46/39c	46/37r
P.R.	San Juan	82/69pc	86/73s	85/72pc	85/71pc
R.I.	Providence	33/32c	39/35r	43/36r	47/37c
S.C.	Greenville	56/46c	65/50pc	75/53pc	67/52sh
	Charleston	67/56pc	75/60s	80/62pc	71/59sh
S.D.	Rapid City	37/30sn	43/30s	43/30c	40/30sh
	Sioux Falls	28/23sn	29/20c	31/20c	31/22c
Tenn.	Memphis	61/51c	74/59sh	68/53c	66/48pc
	Nashville	59/48c	70/55c	68/49sh	63/45pc
Texas	Dallas	76/55c	50/38c	54/34pc	60/38s
	El Paso	68/45s	69/32s	69/30s	72/34s
	Houston	86/62c	69/48r	60/44pc	74/55s
	San Antonio	87/67pc	74/48s	68/48s	74/50s
Utah	Cedar City	46/22pc	53/35pc	57/35c	52/32sh
	Salt Lake City	46/33pc	53/38pc	55/38c	50/35sh
Vermont	Burlington	28/14c	31/27i	38/33c	40/33c
	Rutland	32/31c	30/27i	38/31c	40/33c
Va.	Norfolk	56/37c	53/44pc	63/54pc	52/44sh
	Richmond	56/37c	53/44pc	63/49pc	48/39sh
W.Va.	Charleston	51/43c	50/38pc	59/47pc	53/42c
	Parkersburg	49/39c	54/45c	60/48r	56/46c
Wis.	Eau Claire	36/15s	34/26c	36/31sn	36/29sh
	Milwaukee	31/27c	34/30c	36/33r	36/33sh
Wyoming	Casper	42/31sn	47/32c	49/34sh	46/30sh
	Cheyenne	35/26sn	43/30c	46/34sh	46/30sh

Storm rumbles east

A storm that produced a blizzard in Colorado and Kansas and severe storms in Texas and Oklahoma Sunday will move eastward today and Tuesday. It will spread rain across most of the USA's eastern half, with snow on the storm's northern edge.

Areas affected by storm today and Tuesday

Today

By Ann LaRose and George Rorick, USA TODAY

Thunderstorms, snow hammer midsection

Winter's final weekend dealt the Plains a double dose of trouble Sunday as violent thunderstorms pounded Texas and Oklahoma while a near-blizzard howled through eastern Colorado and western Kansas.

The giant storm system that produced the heavy snow and thunderstorms also spewed sleet and freezing rain across much of Kansas, icing roads and snapping power lines.

■ At midafternoon Manhattan, Kan., reported thundershowers, snow, sleet, freezing rain and fog — all occurring within the same hour.

■ Baseball-size hail knocked out windows in buildings and cars in Parker County west of Fort Worth, Texas.

■ In eastern Colorado, snow — up to 12 inches in places — and winds gusting to 40 mph cut visibility to zero. At least 10 highways, including a 100-mile stretch of Interstate 70 in Colorado and Kansas, were closed.

■ Wind gusts hit 50 mph in northeastern New Mexico, where blowing snow triggered a series of accidents that closed Interstate 25.

■ A tornado in a rural area

northwest of Dallas smashed barns and uprooted trees, but no one was injured.

Today the storm is expected to dump rain on much of the Ohio Valley and sock the Southeast with thunderstorms. Snow and sleet could spread across parts of Iowa and Wisconsin.

Sunday was a gloomy one for most of the USA's eastern half — damp and cloudy, with showers and drizzle in northern Appalachians and freezing drizzle along the southern New England coastline to Boston.

A bright exception was Florida, where temperatures climbed into the 80s under sunny skies.

In the West, a weak storm came ashore in Oregon and Washington, bringing snow to the mountains and rain to lower elevations.

EXTREMES YESTERDAY

Low temperature: Minus 3, Hibbing, Minn.

High temperature: 96 in Tulia, Texas.

AREA WEATHER CLOSE-UP
Call local telephone numbers listed below for more details.

404-767-1784 ATLANTA
Partly sunny and warm, high 73, low 56.
Tomorrow: variable clouds, thunderstorm, high 76, low 56.

Cloudy
may break to allow sunshine, high 52, low 38.
Tomorrow: variable cloudy with drizzle, high 57, low 41.

Cloudy
chilly, periods of rain and drizzle, high 36, low 34.
Tomorrow: mostly cloudy with drizzle, high 40, low 36.

216-931-1212 CLEVELAND
Cloudy
rain or wet snow by night, high 39, low 33.
Tomorrow: rain, high 45, low 36.

Variable clouds
not as cold, high 44, low 34.
Tomorrow: milder, chance of rain, high 53, low 40.

Mostly cloudy
windy and chilly, high 50, low 38.
Tomorrow: partly sunny, brisk and cool, high 54, low 34.

303-936-1212 DENVER
Partly cloudy
and chilly, high 43, low 30.
Tomorrow: mostly sunny, high 53, low 33.

Variable clouds
high 39, low 32.
Tomorrow: chance of rain, high 48, low 40.

713-228-8703 HOUSTON
Thunderstorms
then partly sunny, high 69, low 48.
Tomorrow: mostly sunny, low 50.

816-471-4840 KANSAS CITY
Cloudy
windy, rain or snow, high 38, low 32.
Tomorrow: cloudy, drizzle or snow, low 30.

213-554-1212 LOS ANGELES
Sunny
high 76, low 52.
Tomorrow: sunny, high 74, low 52.

505-661-5065 MPLS.-ST.P.
Mostly sunny
and warm, high 82, low 45.
Tomorrow: mostly sunny and warm, high 82, low 66.

612-452-2202 MPLS.-ST.P.
Partly cloudy
high 39, low 25.
Tomorrow: partly cloudy, high 39, low 27.

504-525-5831 NEW ORLEANS
Thunderstorms
with gusty winds, high 75, low 52.
Tomorrow: windy and cool with some sunshine, high 64, low 50.

212-976-1212 NEW YORK
Cloudy
with drizzle, high 44, low 37.
Tomorrow: cloudy, high 48, low 40.

215-936-1212 PHILADELPHIA
Cloudy
some sunshine, high 48, low 37.
Tomorrow: variable cloudiness with a bit milder, high 55, low 40.

602-273-7511 PHOENIX
Sunny
high 80, low 53.
Tomorrow: sunny, high 82, low 55.

Variable clouds
high 50, low 38.
Tomorrow: cloudy, chance of rain arriving, high 60, low 44.

314-926-1198 ST. LOUIS
Rainy
and breezy, maybe a thunderstorm, high 45, low 34.
Tomorrow: cloudy with lingering drizzle, high 40, low 32.

SALT LAKE
Partly cloudy
high 53, low 38.
Tomorrow: mostly cloudy, high 55, low 38.

415-936-1212 SAN FRAN.
Partly cloudy
high 64, low 52.
Tomorrow: partly cloudy, high 62, low 49.

Rainy
high 59, low 46.
Tomorrow: mostly cloudy with a couple showers, high 56, low 43.

813-645-2900 TAMPA-ST.P.
Mostly sunny
and warm, high 82, low 62.
Tomorrow: partly sunny, late thunderstorm possible, high 82, low 60.

Cloudy
some sunshine, high 53, low 42.
Tomorrow: variable clouds and milder, high 58, low 45.

YESTERDAY'S WORLD WEATHER

Acapulco	91/71pc	London	43/35pc
Athens	60/43pc	Madrid	46/30pc
Berlin	38/32pc	Manila	84/71pc
Buenos Aires	72/60s	Mexico City	81/44s
Cairo	73/54s	Montreal	27/18c
Copenhagen	35/25w	Moscow	24/13sn
Dublin	39/36r	Nassau	86/70s
Geneva	52/32s	New Delhi	82/71s
Hong Kong	76/60pc	Paris	43/35c
Jerusalem	50/40c	Rio de Janeiro	50/45r
Kingston	86/68pc	Rome	28/18s
Lima	75/68pc	Stockholm	48/40s
		Sydney	78/66pc
		Tokyo	27/21c
		Toronto	45/35c
		Vienna	

EXTENDED FORECAST

Pacific Coast: The south will stay mostly sunny and nice through Thursday. There will be showers Tuesday in the north and, after some clearing Wednesday, more showers are possible Thursday.

Rockies: Snow and rain will move from the northwest Tuesday to central sections Wednesday and the east Thursday. The southwest will be sunny.

South Central: Clouds and showers will end Tuesday in the east as it turns a bit cooler. Wednesday will be mostly sunny and pleasant. Thursday will be warmer.

North Central: Tuesday will be partly to mostly cloudy. There's a chance of snow flurries Wednesday and Thursday in the north.

Midwest: Some snow will fall Tuesday from southern Wisconsin to northern Michigan with rain and showers far-

ther south. Wednesday the east will have showers. Thursday will be partly cloudy.

Southeast: There will be showers and thunderstorms in central sections Tuesday and steadier rain in the northeast Thursday may bring showers to the far east.

Northeast: Rain will develop tomorrow afternoon in the southwest and spread Wednesday. Thursday will be partly cloudy with a shower possible.

Weather

Often derided for inaccurate forecasts, the weatherperson has at least pushed the boundaries of graphics on television. The science of forecasting is, by its nature, inexact. Yet news shows always have a weather segment. Don't you long for the presenter, just once, to say: "I haven't got a clue what it will be like outside tomorrow, so tonight I'm giving up my time. Back to the news."

In print, *USA Today* faced our apparently insatiable desire for information—right or wrong—about the weather by devoting their whole back page to maps, tables, explanatory diagrams, and listings of temperatures across the United States and around the world. And they did it in color. In so doing, they changed print reporting of the weather, in the same way that the cult of the television weatherperson (and the computer) changed the way broadcasters spin their tales of *possible precipitation* (what's wrong with saying that "it might rain"?).

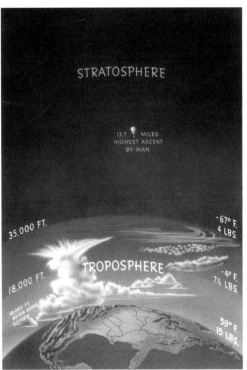

From a 1945 U.S. government booklet The Realm of Flight, *this is an illustration of the troposphere, the lowest (6–12 miles high) layer of earth's atmosphere, in which most cloud formations occur.*

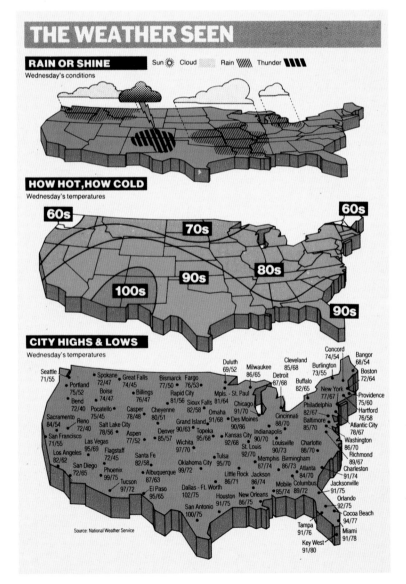

In this national weather graphic for a proposed newspaper syndication service, three layers give an overall picture of sun and clouds, then broad bands of temperatures, and finally, specific locations with high and low readings.

135

George Rorick developed the weather map in *USA Today*, and it certainly was a revolution. The paper was going into the subject in far more detail than anyone had before. They explained such weather-related phenomena as how hurricanes start, or what causes thunder, and they did it, and still do it, very well. In his book *Information Anxiety*, Richard Saul Wurman mildly criticizes the paper for telling you only about the weather and not "about comparative comfort, which is really what you want to know when you look at a weather map." His suggestion is to replace the bands of color representing temperature with bands representing a comfort index, that is, how far above or below a comfortable norm are current conditions. It's an intriguing notion that raises the question of how we use such graphics. Do we understand that the same temperature in two different places will feel different? We do, and we make the necessary mental, and clothing, adjustments. With time it may be possible to educate people so that they can read weather information more

North and South America (left) and Saudi Arabia, the east coast of Africa, the Indian Ocean, and Australia (right) just visible at five o'clock. Beautiful and sobering views of ourselves.

accurately, but only if the information is *correct* when they read it. The success of Wurman's idea relies on there being good data available, for without that any forecasting has to be so generalized as to be almost worthless at the daily, local level.

Apart from jazzing up the graphics on television, computers are having an impact on ideas about weather patterns. At Carnegie-Mellon University, a Cray supercomputer has been used to simulate the smog build-up over Los Angeles. By combining base maps of the area with data on chemical activity in the atmosphere, and by overlaying simple graphic arrows and shapes, they can build a picture of the problem. The same programming can be applied to the effects of smoke from fires in a nuclear war. Just how soon would the sun's rays be shut off by the blanket of smoke, cooling the earth and leading to scientist Carl Sagan's predictions of a nuclear winter? If we can get the computer folks off such scary war scenarios, these programs could be the answer to more down-to-earth questions like "can I plan my picnic for next weekend?"

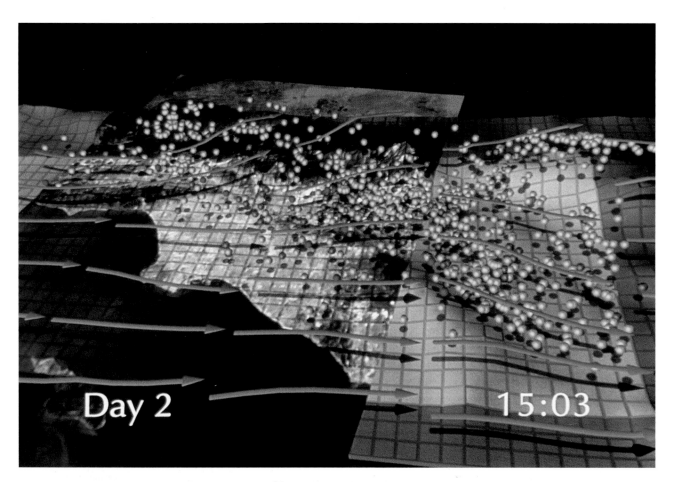

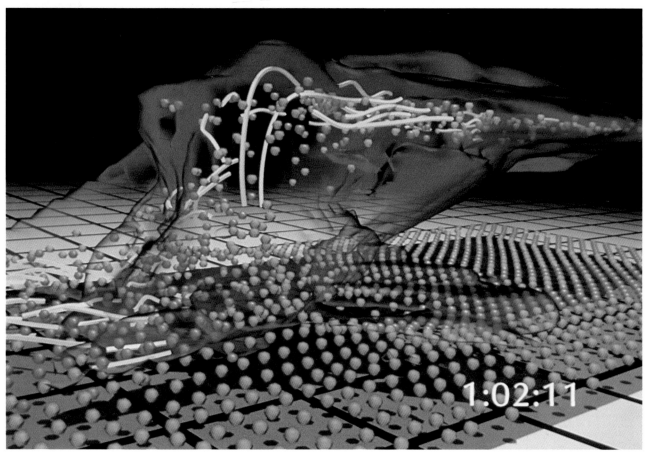

A National Oceanic and Atmospheric satellite photo (right) of conditions over the United States on July 8, 1980. This shot shows clear skies over most of the nation. Heavy thunderstorms can be seen from Northern Virginia to Pennsylvania and also from Nebraska northward to Montana. Pictures like this are released daily to the press. Some papers print them along with their own detailed local map.

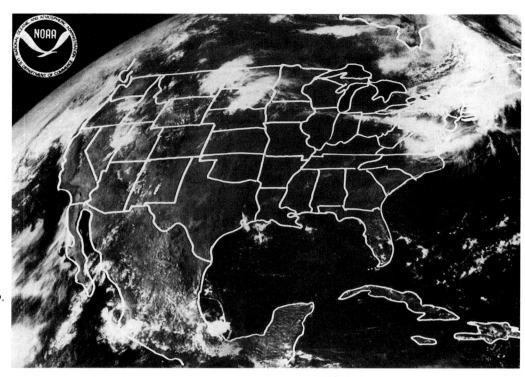

Pictures from space remind us that early cartographers made accurate maps without such aids. This U.S. airforce view of Europe shows an uncharacteristically cloud-free shot of the British Isles.

A computer-colored satellite view by the National Research Centre in Farnborough, England, clearly shows the ravages of a prevailing west-wind weather system on the northwest coast of Scotland and on the fjord-cracked western coast of Norway.

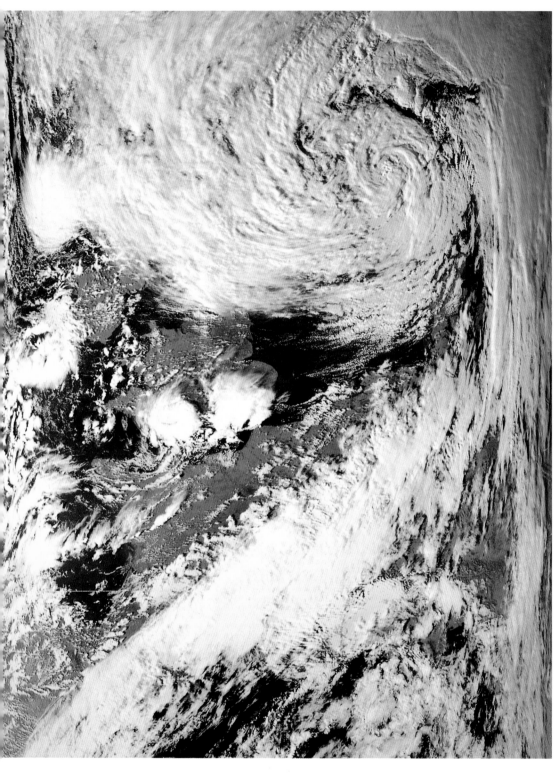

A color computer-enhanced satellite picture of the hurricane that hit southeast England on October 16, 1987, causing terrible damage to structures and especially to trees. Two clumps of white clouds remain over the south coast, and the center of the storm has moved east, to Scandinavia. Central parts of England and Ireland can be seen through the clouds.

6

Doing It

Projections made easy
Drawing mountains
Symbols
The computer
Scale

We have seen examples of mapmakers and artists drawing the world in a variety of different ways. Whether or not they knew it when they were drawing, they used methods of visualizing the world that are well cataloged. These basic principles of mapmaking apply to the creation of scientific maps, but they also need to be understood by anyone who is serious about this job, even though they may be setting out to *illustrate* more than to *map*. Six subjects are covered below: projections made understandable; ways of drawing mountains; the use of symbols; the computer's contribution; what is revealed by a comparison of the scale of different countries; and statistical "views of the world" that distort the real geographic shapes of countries.

Before you can take liberties with anything, you should learn the rules that you might be about to break. This is particularly the case when it comes to using the most basic part of cartography— the projection for the base-map on which to build the information you want to show.

Problems with Projections

The big problem for cartographers has always been how to draw, on a flat surface, shapes that actually exist on a sphere. I explain below some of the different ways that mapmakers have tried to solve this eternal puzzle.

When you peel an orange, you can understand why it's so hard to draw the earth. The peel won't lie flat. Map projection is the science of wrestling the orange peel into submission: it is the translation of the surface of a three-dimensional sphere into a two-dimensional map. More than two hundred ways to do this have been published, and that large number reflects the problem: No single projection does everything. Some are good for one job, but useless for another. A projection can show one of these three properties: the correct *scale*; the correct *area*; or the correct *direction*—but never all three at the same time.

When Mercator produced his famous projection in 1569, he was fulfilling the needs of navigators. He created a map that allowed them to plot their course as a straight line between two points, however distant. His projection, however, took care of direction only. The Mercator map thus misleads us when it comes to presenting a true view of the world; the scale differs from one part of the map to another, and the land areas are badly distorted. To make matters worse, the Mercator projection is the one most commonly used in atlases, schoolrooms, and behind television news broadcasters, so we see it more often than any other. It has become our accepted view of the world to the extent that other projections don't look quite right.

(Opposite page) The orange peel won't lie flat. That's cartography's unsolvable problem, and it is the reason why so many projections have been developed to represent the surface of the earth in two dimensions.

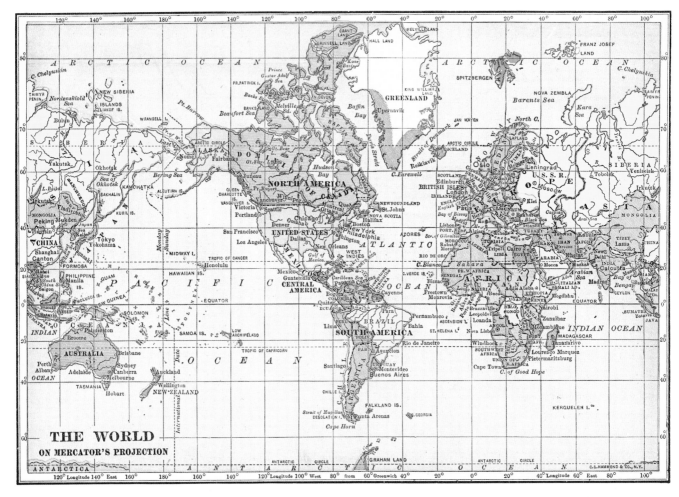

THE WORLD

ON MERCATOR'S PROJECTION

Mercator's projection, first published in 1569, allowed navigators to plot their course as a straight line, but it exaggerated landmasses in north and south latitudes.

A		A
B		B
C		C
D		D
E		E
F		F
G		G
H		H
I		I

Latitude lines are shorter the nearer they are to the poles (left). Mercator's map necessitated latitude lines of equal length (right), thus stretching out what are in fact single points (the poles) to a line of the same length as the equator. This is why landmasses in the north and south are enlarged on Mercator's map.

The problem with Mercator's map is that, in order to permit the sailor to keep a true compass bearing as a straight line, Mercator had to stretch out the landmasses as they approached the North and South poles. He drew lines of latitude (east to west) and longitude (north to south) as straight lines and at right angles to one another, converting all the lines of latitude to the same length, when in reality they are not (they get shorter toward the poles). Mercator knew that this square-edged grid made it impossible for him to draw the polar regions—he had stretched out the single point at which the pole occurs to a line the same length as the equator (he dealt with the problem by supplying a separate, inset view of the North Polar area on his map).

The distortion inherent in Mercator's map is the reason we think that Greenland is huge, larger than South America, when it is really only about the size of Mexico; that Alaska and Brazil appear to be the same size, when in fact Brazil is almost six times as large (sorry about that, Alaska); and that Africa is smaller than North America, when it is two million square miles larger.

In January 1990, the American Cartographic Association (ACA) issued a paper urging book and map publishers, the media, and government agencies to abandon all square-gridded,

142

rectangular maps in favor of rounded ones. In so doing, the ACA was addressing the rising tide of objections to the landmass misrepresentations of the Mercator projection. In the great man's defense, it should be restated that his work was never meant to show land areas. In Mercator's time, the sea captains for whom the map was specifically drawn had little need to sail in the extreme northern and southern regions of the earth and so were not concerned by the land distortions that this projection showed in those areas. What Mercator did was absolutely necessary for efficient navigation in his own time, and it is still used today for that purpose.

The four common rectangular maps that came under fire from the ACA were Mercator's (drawn in 1569), Gall's (1855), Miller's (1942) and Gall-Peters's (1967). Not only did they distort the shapes and sizes of landmasses, which led to misunderstandings about world relationships, but they also visually betrayed the fact that the world is spherical.

One of these projections, the German cartographer Arno Peters's adaption of the Gall map of 1855, is an attempt to correct some of the distortions of the Mercator map, which was Europe-centered and which diminished the size of the southern hemisphere, affecting mostly third world countries. Arthur Robinson, often referred to as the dean of American cartography, described the Gall-Peters map as making the world look like ''wet, ragged, long winter underwear hung out to dry on the Arctic circle.'' and as it would be seen ''in a fun-house mirror.'' This map tried to redress the *size* distortions of the continents, but ended up using *shape* distortions.

We are conditioned by prior mental images. It will take a lot to change our view of the world; that's what Robinson meant when he referred to Peters's map as *looking* like something other than our expected view. He is right to object on aesthetic grounds, but we will never find the perfect answer to the projection puzzle.

The graphic artist must be aware of the questions raised by a particular projection used as a base-map. If world maps are to be used as any more than a background on which to plant descriptive pictorial information, then the artist should consider the relationships of the continents. Obviously a map of the incidence of AIDS in the world will look a certain way if the Peters projection is used—Africa's *size* (and therefore relative visual importance) on the map will match the magnitude of the horror there—but remember, it's not really that *shape*, even though its *mass* is correct.

Regardless of whether he did it well, Peters was at least trying to get us to take notice of the real continental relationships of the world, which were not being properly shown on the most

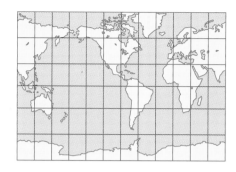

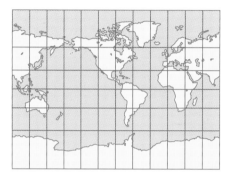

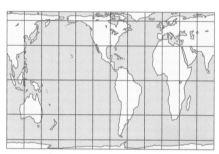

Rectangular projections: Gall's projection, 1855 (top); Miller's projection, 1942 (center); Gall-Peters' projection, 1967 (bottom). These three, together with Mercator's projection, have been attacked by the American Cartographic Association as poor representations of the world's landmasses.

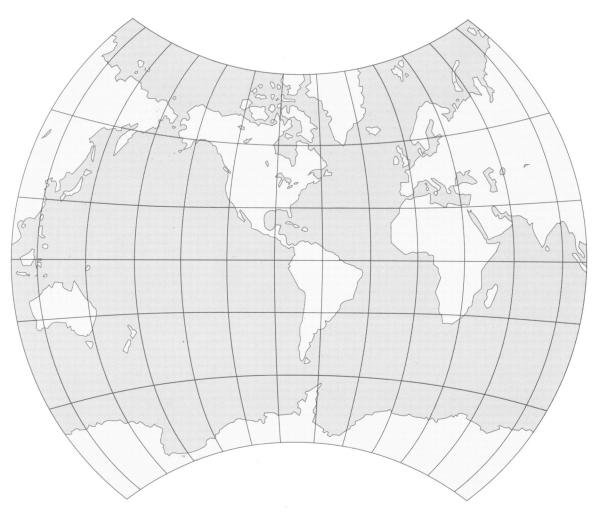

The Van der Grinten projection (above) was used by the National Geographic Society from 1922 until 1988. Landmasses in the north and south are exaggerated. The Soviet Union is 225 percent larger than in reality—it appears to be larger than Africa. Greenland is 550 percent larger than it should be.

The Robinson projection (below) developed in 1963, was adopted by Rand McNally and later (1988) by the National Geographic Society. In comparison with Van der Grinten's projection, the Soviet Union appears only 18 percent larger than its true size, while Greenland appears 60 percent larger.

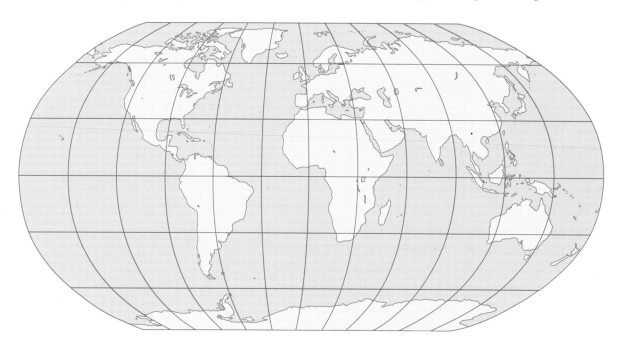

commonly used maps. Getting us to look differently at the world was also the subject of a terrific essay by Richard Edes Harrison in *Look at the World*. Harrison argues that we are conditioned to look at maps in one way only. We do this because of the northern orientation of most maps. As we have seen, in medieval times the East was at the top of most maps. Later on with the more-or-less regular use of the equator as a *horizontal*, east-west line, the North naturally took its place at the top of maps, but Harrison makes the point that this is exactly what has led to our fixed view of geography. Try some tests to prove to yourself that you do have a built-in viewpoint. Turn a letter of the alphabet, or a face, or a map upside down, and see how odd it looks and how different; yet do the same thing with a pair of scissors and the effect is not the same. That's because the scissors are not generally seen from one viewpoint, so they look just fine from any angle. If we were to apply the same free-floating principle to maps, we'd find that it reveals lots about the world that remains hidden in the conventional view, simply because it is the conventional view—we are not really looking at the map in the first place. (We are merely being reminded of something we had "seen" many times before.) This is similar to the effect of holding up a drawing to the light and looking at it through the back of the paper. You can see the faults in the work by forcing yourself to look at it unconventionally—in this case, backward.

As Harrison says, "turning maps in new directions helps us to get out of the totally unnecessary straitjacket of geographical fixations." To clarify this point, Harrison uses the example of the map of Italy. In general, we think of Italy as running roughly north to south; in fact, it has a decidedly eastward swing.

Down-To-Earth Stuff

Before detailing different projections, here are some basic facts.

The surface area of the earth is 197 million square miles. Three-fifths of this is covered with water; all the continents together would fit into an area the size of the Pacific Ocean.

Latitude is the distance north or south of the equator. It is measured in degrees from 0° to 90°, north or south. Each degree is divided into sixty minutes (60′), and each minute into sixty seconds (60″). The latitude for New York City is expressed as 40° 40′N; London, 53° 30′N; Moscow, 55° 45′N. Each degree of latitude is about sixty-nine miles apart.

Longitude is the distance east or west of a line running from the North Pole to the South Pole through Greenwich, England. This is the Greenwich meridian (hence Greenwich Mean Time, time zones, and so on). New York City is 73° 58′W; London, 0° 10′W; Moscow, 37° 42′E. At the equator, lines of longitude

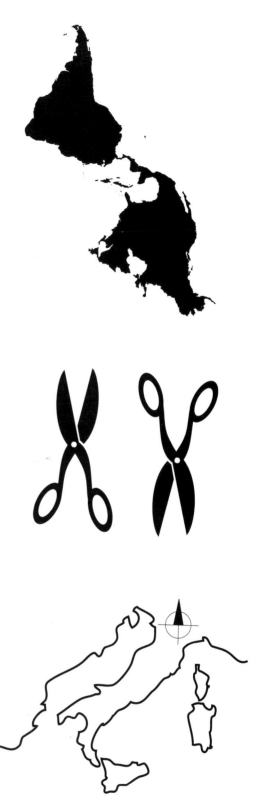

Take a different look at the world: new relationships are noticed when the map is turned upside down; but it doesn't work with a pair of scissors because we have no prior mental viewpoint fixed in our minds. Italy has more of a tilt to the east than we would have thought. It's more visible when we see it reversed.

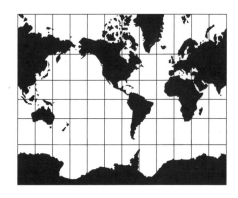

Mercator's (top) and Lambert's (bottom) projections are conformal *projections.*

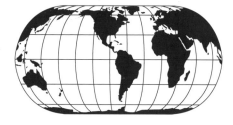

Mollweide's (top) and Eckert's (bottom) projections are equal-area *projections.*

are widest apart (1° is about seventy miles there), and the lines come closer together north and south of the equator until they join at the poles.

Any position on earth can be expressed in terms of its latitude and longitude. The complete grid placement of New York City is thus: 40° 40′N, 73° 58′W. Look it up in an atlas.

Two Types of Projections

There are two broad categories of projections: *conformal* and *equal-area*.

A *conformal map* presents small individual sections of the earth with internal details shown correctly, and land shapes the same as they appear on the globe. Over a larger area these do not have the same scale. Examples of conformal maps are the Mercator map and Lambert's conic map. Conformal maps are good for finding direction (navigation) and bad for scale.

An *equal-area map* gives the correct size relationships to landmasses but has to distort their shape to do so. Examples of equal-area maps are those by Mollweide or Eckert. These maps are good for showing the relative sizes of countries (and therefore for showing distribution of products or comparisons of economic statistics) and bad for showing the actual shapes of countries.

(Since no map is perfect, yet commerce and science need to coexist in the simplest graphic way, *compromise* projections have developed, combining parts of the two main groups. An example of a compromise map is Robinson's map [see page 000].)

Three Ways To Create Projections

Erwin Raisz in *General Cartography* defines a projection as ''any orderly system of parallels and meridians on which a map can be drawn.'' The term *projection* originally referred to a system of projecting geographical shapes (which were etched on a glass globe) onto a flat surface. A light source was set up inside the globe, and the resulting cast shadows were traced on the flat plane. Thus something that existed in the round was transformed into a two-dimensional image. It is easy to imagine how the image from the edges of the globe became distorted when it reached the paper. Projections are named for both the particular inventor and the three-dimensional shape that was used as the starting point. The finished two-dimensional projections fall into three basic groups: those that use a cylinder of paper as the starting point to transform the sphere into a flat plane, those that use a cone of paper, and those that use a flat piece of paper. Modern projections are actually mathematical and are not done by shining a light through a glass globe and laboriously tracing

the result on a sheet of paper, but it is helpful to visualize the
process in more concrete terms, such as those outlined below.

1. Cylindrical projections   Imagine a globe inside a piece of
paper rolled around it like a tube. Only the complete circle of the
circumference of the globe touches the cylinder of paper (dotted
line in illustration). The grid from the globe is projected onto the
inside surface of the tube, which is then unrolled and laid flat.
Slightly different projections are produced if point x is positioned
on the back of the globe (this is called a *cylindrical stereographic*
projection), or in the center of the globe (*simple cylindrical*), or is
in fact not one point, but many (*cylindrical orthographic*).
Mercator is in this category.

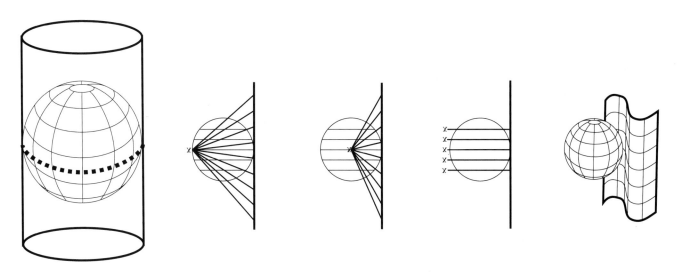

2. Conic projections   Imagine a globe wearing a dunce's hat.
One parallel of the grid touches the cone (dotted line in
illustration). The grid is projected onto the cone, which is then
spread out into a fan shape.

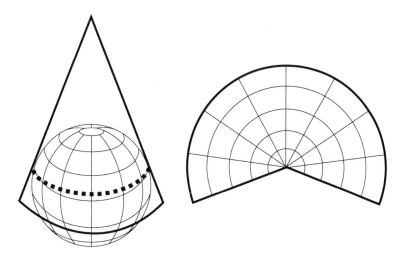

3. Flat plane projection (usually referred to as azimuthal projection)

3. Flat plane projection (usually referred to as azimuthal projection) Imagine a globe wearing a scholar's mortar board. Only one point of the globe touches the plane (the North Pole in this illustration). The grid is projected onto the flat plane.

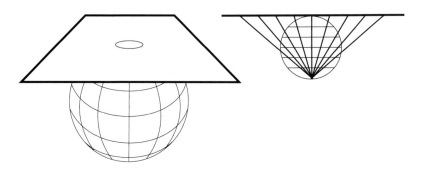

Goode's interrupted *projection.*

One variant deserves notice. The oddly-shaped *interrupted* projection, or homosoline (equal-area), by J. Paul Goode, drawn in 1923 (which is actually a cylindrical projection) preserves the relative spacing and shapes of the continents and has a certain ring of truth that reminds us of attempts to make the orange peel lie flat. But because of the broken up (interrupted) oceans, we do not see it as a representation of the globe; it is more a diagram than a map. In our mind's eye we can easily bend back the tongues of sea and join them together into a sphere, even though they are not pictured that way.

At a time when the world political situation seems to be less threatening, it is particularly appropriate that the National Geographic Society has changed its base for most world maps from the Van der Grinten projection, in use since 1922, to the more "accurate" Robinson projection, devised in 1963. By adopting the Van der Grinten, the society had begun the move away from Mercator. In 1988 they made the next move, changing to the compromise projection by Robinson, which goes a long way to correcting the Greenland and Africa size problems, and also cuts the USSR down to size (in a nice reflection of the end of the cold war).

Solve your world projection quandary with a globe. But if you want detail, I hope you've got enough room for a big globe. Take Sicily, for example: Richard Harrison points out that to see the World War II military operations there, you would need a detailed map three feet wide. A globe of that scale would be 150 feet in diameter. On a regular household globe, with an eighteen-inch diameter, Sicily is only three-eighths of an inch wide.

Aware of the distortions in other, mathematically formulated projections, Robinson started by drawing the landmasses the way he knew them to exist on the globe, and only then did he find a mathematical formula with which to project them. By working "backwards . . . with a kind of artistic approach," Arthur Robinson has produced a map that is the best that cartography can currently do in its quest for a solution to the impossible job of drawing all surfaces of a sphere at once. The globe retains that trophy, for now.

Relief

Drawing Mountains   In making a map with bumps on it, you can go two ways. The first way is to draw a perspective picture, a true view of the area, hills and all, as though it were seen from an angle up in the air. This representation is more like a picture than a true map, for you have to distort the ground as it recedes away from you in order to give the impression of distance. The second way is to take a regular plan map and put symbols on it to represent mountains. Relief maps can be drawn in many ways, but they all fall into one of these two categories. The mountains on the first type of map could be the same as those on the second type, but the first will always be a *picture*. The second is primarily a *map*, and a picture only as an afterthought. This section is about drawing bumps on whatever type of map.

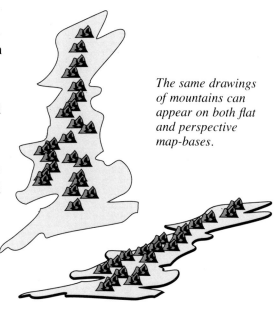

The same drawings of mountains can appear on both flat and perspective map-bases.

Hillocks   Until the end of the eighteenth century the standard forms for relief on maps were hillocks. These hillocks first appeared on early maps, but they were exemplified by Mercator and Speed in the late sixteenth and early seventeenth centuries. The maps of these two great cartographers often looked remarkably similar, and this was no coincidence, as Speed sent his work over to Holland to be engraved by the best craftsman of the period, Jodocus Hondius, who also became one of Mercator's engravers. One side of each little hill was shaded with diagonal lines to give an impression of solidity, but not much attention was given to height or position. They were very general hills, without a real system of accountability to accuracy.

Hillocks of the type Mercator and Speed used on their maps.

Hachures   In 1799, an Austrian army officer called Lehmann proposed a new method of drawing relief features on a map. This method used *hachures*, a series of little lines that followed the direction of the slope of hills. By varying the width of the lines, the steepness of the slope could be indicated. The steeper the slope, the darker the line, until the incline had reached 45 degrees or more, when the lines joined into a black mass. This was difficult to draw well, and many examples deteriorated into what Arthur Robinson has called "woolly worms."

Hachures replaced the shaded hillocks, but often became overworked and looked like "wooly worms," obscuring the lettering.

There were three problems associated with the hachure method: first, flat areas of land appeared the same whether they were at the top of a hill or in a valley below; second, if the map was reproduced in one color, and it usually was—black—the lettering was very hard to read over the mass of engraved lines; third, a great deal of information about the terrain was needed for an artist to produce the map. Often this information was not available in enough detail to make the method worthwhile. Quite a difference, though, from the unscientific hills of before: Suddenly there was too much information on the map.

Contour lines were a more accurate representation of the topography, but they didn't look like hills and valleys.

Illuminated contours *filled in the spaces between contours to give a better impression of the landscape.*

How to draw shaded relief maps

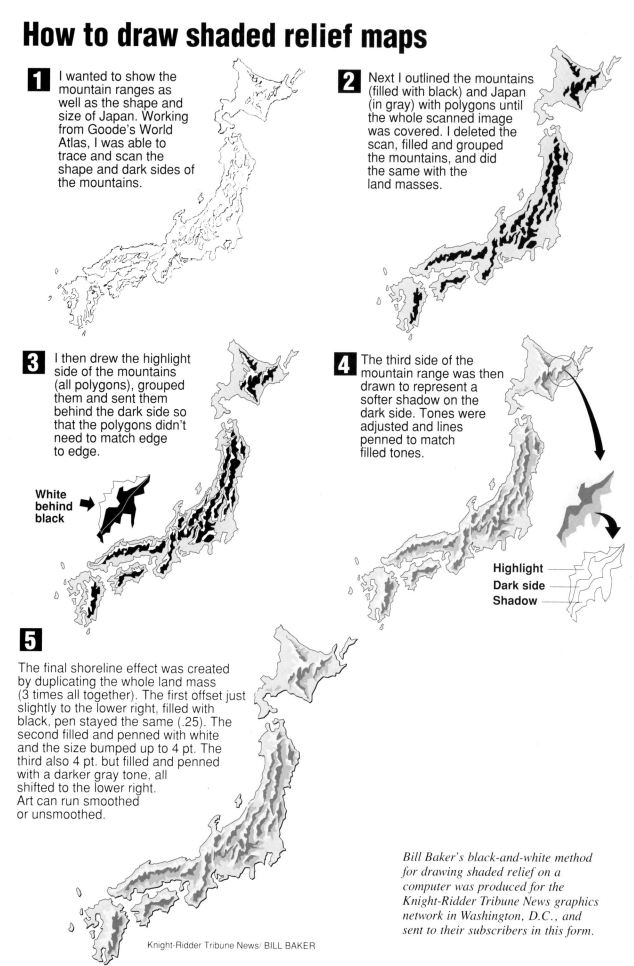

1 I wanted to show the mountain ranges as well as the shape and size of Japan. Working from Goode's World Atlas, I was able to trace and scan the shape and dark sides of the mountains.

2 Next I outlined the mountains (filled with black) and Japan (in gray) with polygons until the whole scanned image was covered. I deleted the scan, filled and grouped the mountains, and did the same with the land masses.

3 I then drew the highlight side of the mountains (all polygons), grouped them and sent them behind the dark side so that the polygons didn't need to match edge to edge.

White behind black

4 The third side of the mountain range was then drawn to represent a softer shadow on the dark side. Tones were adjusted and lines penned to match filled tones.

Highlight
Dark side
Shadow

5

The final shoreline effect was created by duplicating the whole land mass (3 times all together). The first offset just slightly to the lower right, filled with black, pen stayed the same (.25). The second filled and penned with white and the size bumped up to 4 pt. The third also 4 pt. but filled and penned with a darker gray tone, all shifted to the lower right. Art can run smoothed or unsmoothed.

Bill Baker's black-and-white method for drawing shaded relief on a computer was produced for the Knight-Ridder Tribune News graphics network in Washington, D.C., and sent to their subscribers in this form.

Knight-Ridder Tribune News/ BILL BAKER

Contour Lines Originally invented by the Dutch mapmaker Cruquins around 1700 (to represent the bottom of the Merwede River), contour lines did not become common as tools for topographic description until the nineteenth century. In geography, such lines are more properly called *isolines*, or lines that follow the land at equal depth or altitude. It was largely through the efforts of followers of Edmund Halley (of comet fame) that contours became popular. Halley had depicted, using what were to be called *Halleyan lines*, areas of the earth where magnetic variation was equal. Imagine a landscape flooded with dyed water. When the flood recedes, all the land up to the high water mark is left with a line of the dye. Floods of different depths, and with different colors would leave successive marks on the land. The result would be a bit like Arizona's Painted Desert. Contour lines were just that—lines, and although they were more accurate than little hills as methods of showing relief, they gave no impression of what a place actually *looked* like. They were, however, great for statistical studies, and scientists and cartographers began to apply Halley's principles to the study and display of almost any geophysical data, from weather variations to the number of earthquakes along a given line.

In 1842, cartographers began to color in the spaces between contour lines. This showed more clearly than the lines themselves all those areas that were of equal height. But the result was still diagrammatic: There was no *visualization* of height, even though a fairly standard set of colors was commonly used (from blue for the sea, through green and brown and so on, up to purple and white at the top of mountains) so that the mind could be trained to "see" height variations.

In modern times contour-line relief has been taken to its limits in the work of J. Tanaka, who combined hachures and isolines in a method called *illuminated contours*. Tanaka drew hachures between the contour lines to indicate the degree of slope, but then erased the contours themselves, leaving just the pattern of visually descriptive—but also measurably accurate—hachures. Where these hachures ended was left the merest hint of the contour; and the whole was printed in subtle, soft colors so that place-names and other features could be overprinted in a dark color and easily read.

Shading The widespread use of good lithographic color printing in the first half of the nineteenth century made it possible for artists to reproduce continuous shading, but mapmakers did not use this method to depict mountains until 1870, when the first really visual maps of the earth's surface appeared. A superb example of full-color, fully shaded relief can be seen in the

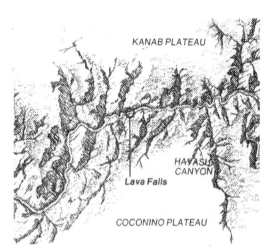

Some places demand heavyweight topographical treatment. This nice pencil drawing of the Grand Canyon is from the New York Times *in 1981.*

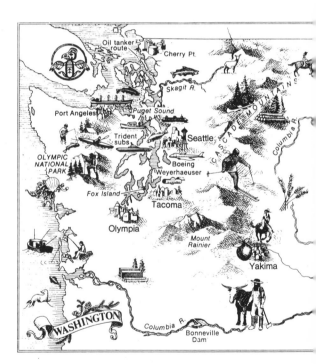

Lazlo Kubinyi's work has a soft precision that is perfect for relief backgrounds.

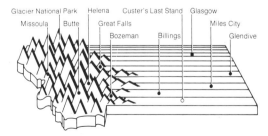

Hard-edged and simplified, this small map of Montana is from the Champion Magazine.

151

A COMPARATIVE View OF THE HEIGHTS OF THE PRINCIPAL MOUNTAINS IN THE WORLD.

Drawn & Eng.ᵈ by R. Scott

This one-view compilation (above) of the world's peaks is from a 1724 atlas. Direct comparisons of geographic features taken out of their normal context in this way make compelling information graphics.

maps published by Raven, a company that bases its images on extremely precise U.S. Geological Survey material. In a separate development of the new age of cartography, the company's artists use computers to produce views of the surface of the earth and the ocean floor by manipulating huge geophysical data bases that are used for minerals exploration.

Exaggeration   Just as we are conditioned to recognize that the shapes of the earth's continents are distorted by the very act of making a map of them, we are also conditioned to accept a huge exaggeration in the size of mountains depicted on top of those landmasses. Terrain cannot be shown true to the size of the earth. The very highest point on earth, Mount Everest, is 29,000 feet high. That's about 5½ miles up. Imagine that distance along the ground. On an average atlas-sized map of India and Nepal, where the scale is perhaps 200 miles to an inch, the correct size of this high point should be not much bigger than a dot. But who can resist graphically celebrating the size of Everest? We want to exaggerate it, and all other hills, for that matter. Why put effort into drawing them if they only come out as tiny pimples with no chance for all that lovely three-dimensional, eye-fooling stuff? So exaggerate. It's not only OK, it's a must, if you want to *see* anything. Talk about making a mountain out of a molehill: It ought to be the other way 'round. A perennial favorite at the Cartographer's Ball is *Ain't No Mountain Low Enough*.

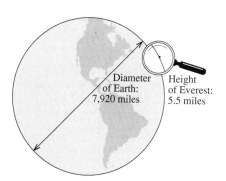

Mount Everest is 29,000 feet high. Compared to the size of the earth, it's a pimple. Exaggerate.

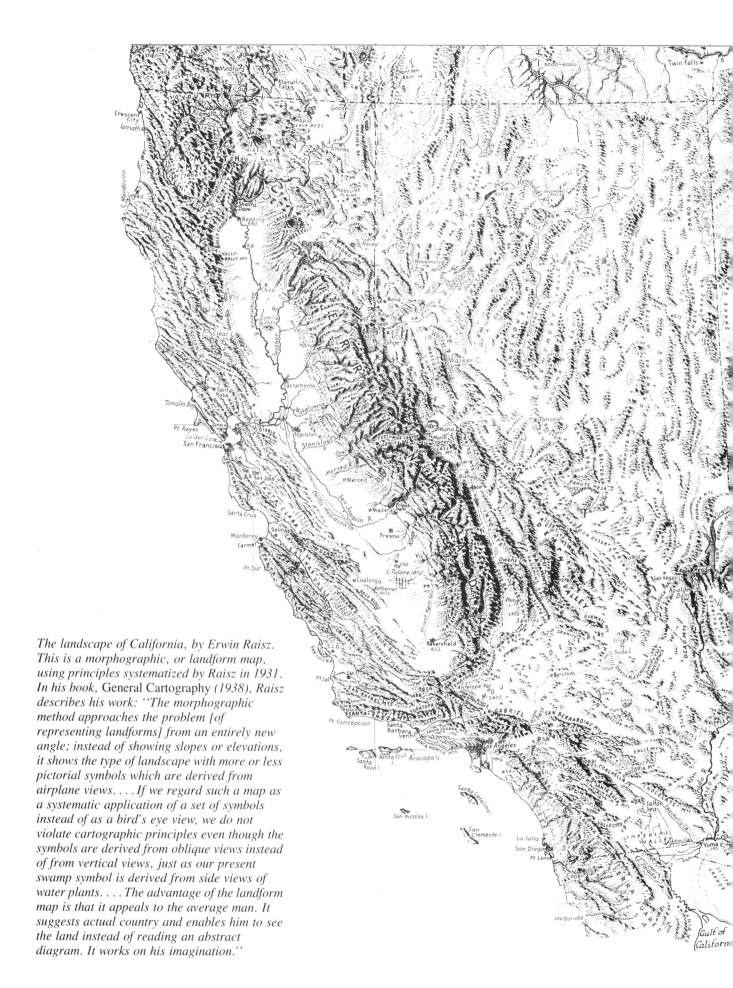

The landscape of California, by Erwin Raisz. This is a morphographic, or landform map, using principles systematized by Raisz in 1931. In his book, General Cartography *(1938), Raisz describes his work: "The morphographic method approaches the problem [of representing landforms] from an entirely new angle; instead of showing slopes or elevations, it shows the type of landscape with more or less pictorial symbols which are derived from airplane views. . . . If we regard such a map as a systematic application of a set of symbols instead of as a bird's eye view, we do not violate cartographic principles even though the symbols are derived from oblique views instead of from vertical views, just as our present swamp symbol is derived from side views of water plants. . . . The advantage of the landform map is that it appeals to the average man. It suggests actual country and enables him to see the land instead of reading an abstract diagram. It works on his imagination."*

153

Symbols

From the earliest days, cartographers realized that they had to simplify in order to represent objects and places on the ground areas shown in their maps. Thus towns became one or two buildings, and hills the characteristic little bumps of the Dutch engraver Hondius. Not only did they simplify, but they disregarded scale. Nowadays we take it for granted that Florida's swamp grass is not ten miles high, and that a railroad is not a mile wide, although if we took the time to measure them, that's what they would be on most maps of the United States. It's only when there are many activities or places to cram onto a map, and they all have to be perfectly readable, do we realize that the size of symbols can badly distort geographical information. How many times have you faced the assignment of drawing a map that needed to show six oil rigs, a bison and a reindeer population, some old gold mines, and a camping site, all surrounding a city? You know that there are exactly six rigs—do you use one symbol for each? You don't know how many bison there are in the area, but you can safely bet on more than six, so you go ahead and correctly put in six oil rigs and one bison (which might represent one hundred). You're making up the rules as you go along. Added to that, the bison move around. Finding a way to make all the symbols cluster around the town is the real problem here. By the time all the commodities, activities, and wildlife are represented, you may have covered 200 square miles on your map for what is really only a 10 square-mile area on the ground. Individual cases must be judged on their merits or faults. Be aware of the problems and you will find ways to solve them. Here, for example, you might cluster all the symbols to the side and use a pointer leading to the exact location of the town on the map. One thing is certain: Symbols, especially pictorial ones, bring life to a map, and you would be amazed how small they can be and still be readable.

The Sunshine State shown as a collection of places to live. This map is from an ad for a group of Florida realtors; symbols and map become one.

In Vienna in the early 1920s, Otto Neurath began formulating ways to display statistics. Hundreds of pictorial symbols like these, from 1935, were developed for him by a team of designers under the direction of Gerd Arntz. Neurath's work is still relevant today.

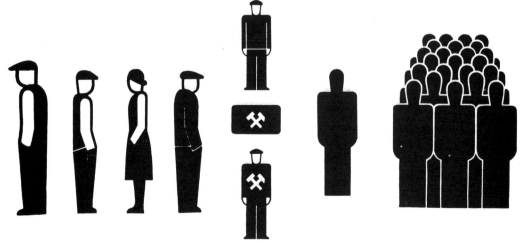

154

In the context of this book, some of the following examples use symbols decoratively—to make up the entire background of a land shape, for instance. Others sit pictorially on the land, and in one example the symbols *are* the map, the outlines of which have disappeared, because the symbolic drawings hold up very well alone.

One of my all-time heroes is Otto Neurath (1882–1945), who developed a pictorial language system called ISOTYPE (International System Of Typographic Picture Education). In 1925 he started the Vienna Museum of Social and Economic Studies, where he and a team of artists produced maps and charts that he hoped could be understood by anyone regardless of language or education. He hired Gerd Arntz, a figurative artist whose work was mainly bold lino cuts, to be the museum's art director. Under Arntz's direction the studio produced literally hundreds of great pictorial symbols that remain useful to this day. At first there were strict limits to the way the artwork was done: only by lino cutting or by using cut paper. This immediately forced the studio artists to simplify their images. Although some of the symbols may be a little out-of-date now, many are not, for they captured the *essence* of a thing and were not a representation of what a thing *looked* like. That is probably as good a definition of a symbol as you need. In England, Neurath's work was continued after his death by his wife, Marie; in the United States, Rudolph Modley produced good work in the same vein and collected many examples of pictorial symbols.

Size, shape, simplicity: the three properties of symbols. Consider these, and the interactions between them, when designing map symbols.

The principles of Otto Neurath were continued in the United States by Rudolf Modley at the Pictograph Corporation of New York. This map of Texas, with its well-balanced arrangement of symbols was designed by the Pictograph Corporation for the World Book Encyclopedia. *The map's design is clear, and the reader is engaged by the clutter of tiny pictures without being faced with too much information.*

A page from Herbert Bayer's World Geo-Graphic Atlas *(1953). In this atlas, both the design and the use of symbols were exemplary; and it was not achieved without extraordinary effort and attention to detail: The project was started in 1948 and took five years to complete.*

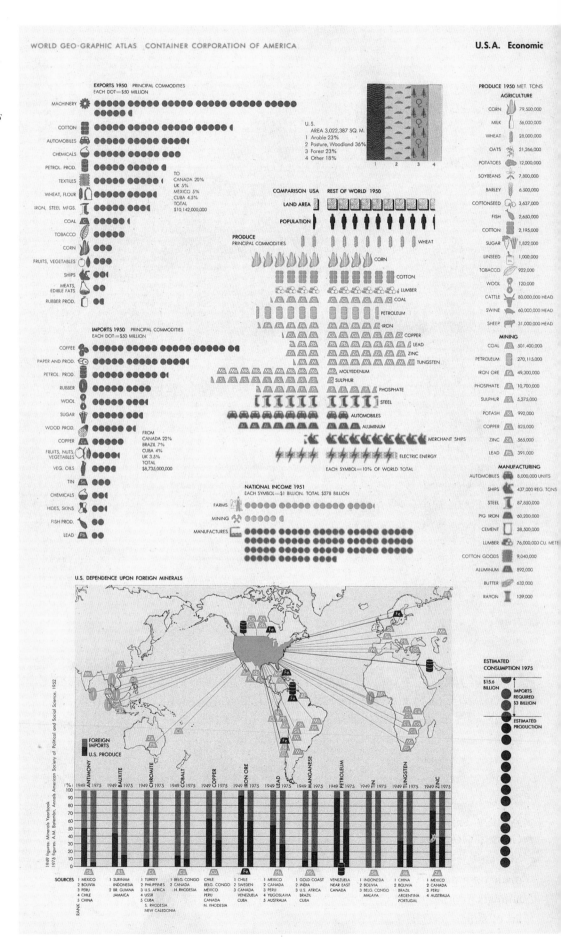

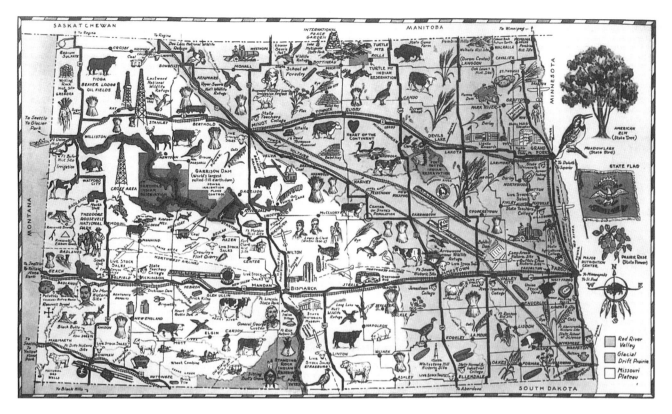

Herbert Bayer's classic *World Geo-Graphic Atlas* was published privately in 1953 by the Container Corporation of America as a giveaway to their clients and as an educational tool for libraries and schools. In it were some of the best and most informative maps ever published, and it set a standard for future commercial atlases. Bayer's use of symbols was based on Neurath's Vienna Method of stacking or lining up many tiny images to represent numbers of people, automobiles, or tons of some commodity produced in a given area. The page reproduced here shows the wealth of symbols he created specially for this project, the careful positioning of the map itself, and the design of the whole page, which is packed with information that begs to be read.

Some symbols stray a little from the strict definition of a graphic mark that represents a generic form or idea—a city, an oil rig, or a nuclear site—and some maps are of cities whose landmarks have become symbols in themselves. In a map of Paris you can't draw a generic tower for the Eiffel Tower, in St. Louis a generic arch, in London a generic clocktower for Big Ben, in Rome a generic coliseum, or in Pisa a generic leaning tower. But you *could* symbolize the whole of London with an upright Grenadier Guardsman, or Paris with an artist in a beret. Similarly, if the variety of Alaska's wildlife is the point to be made on a map, then you must draw accurate symbols of those animals in order to differentiate between them. This is where the art of simplification and selection is important. It's no good just

Published by the Greater North Dakota Association, and drawn by Clell Gannon, this Land of Opportunity map gleefully spreads symbols in an even mix across the state. The same hand that drew the symbols wrote the names, making the map a unified image.

These landmark structures, simply drawn, are more a reminder of what to expect in Paris than they are a map of the city.

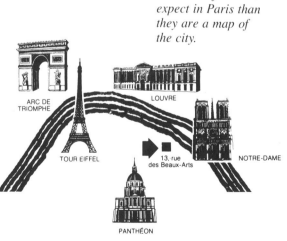

157

*Following the oil-spill
from the* Exxon
Valdez *in 1989,* Time
*ran this map in an
article about the
environmental impact
on Alaska as a whole.
Many different
animals had to be
shown; thus the
symbols needed a
degree of illustrative
reality in order to
distinguish between
them. Note the
comparison between
the size of Alaska and
the U.S. (top, right).*

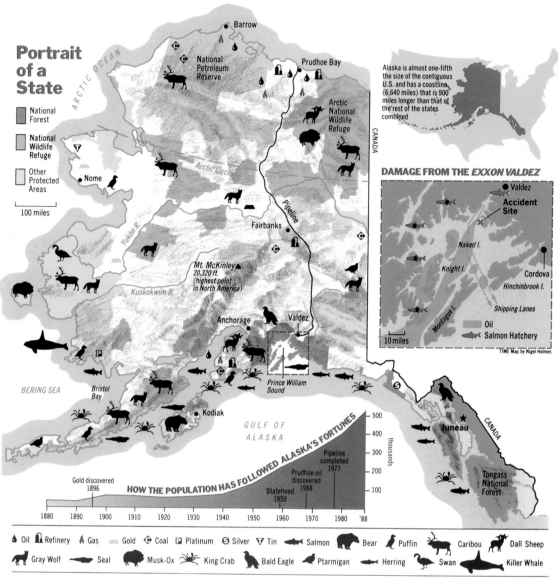

Portrait of a State

National Forest

National Wildlife Refuge

Other Protected Areas

100 miles

Barrow

National Petroleum Reserve

Prudhoe Bay

Arctic National Wildlife Refuge

CANADA

Nome

Arctic Circle

Yukon R.

Fairbanks

Pipeline

Mt. McKinley 20,320 ft. (highest point in North America)

Kuskokwim R.

BERING SEA

Bristol Bay

Anchorage

Valdez

Prince William Sound

Kodiak

GULF OF ALASKA

Juneau

CANADA

Tongass National Forest

Alaska is almost one-fifth the size of the contiguous U.S. and has a coastline (6,640 miles) that is 900 miles longer than that of the rest of the states combined

DAMAGE FROM THE *EXXON VALDEZ*

Valdez

Accident Site

Naked I.

Knight I.

Cordova

Hinchinbrook I.

Shipping Lanes

Montague I.

Oil

Salmon Hatchery

10 miles

TIME Map by Nigel Holmes

HOW THE POPULATION HAS FOLLOWED ALASKA'S FORTUNES

Gold discovered 1896

Statehood 1959

Prudhoe oil discovered 1968

Pipeline completed 1977

thousands — 500 400 300 200 100

1880 1890 1900 1910 1920 1930 1940 1950 1960 1970 1980 '88

Oil | Refinery | Gas | Gold | Coal | Platinum | Silver | Tin | Salmon | Bear | Puffin | Caribou | Dall Sheep

Gray Wolf | Seal | Musk-Ox | King Crab | Bald Eagle | Ptarmigan | Herring | Swan | Killer Whale

*Lance Wyman's symbols for the Mexico
Olympic Games in 1968 (and soccer's World
Cup held there in 1970) raised the design of
signage and sports logos to a new level. Here is
part of his map of the Mexico City subway
system. A different pictorial symbol was
designed to represent a landmark near each
stop on a subway line. A string of symbols then
became* the subway line *on the map.*

to trace the outline from a photo in the hope that the drawing will
look like the animal. Without internal shading or pattern, you
may not understand what the outline stands for. Use the photo as
reference by all means, but try to draw the symbol from scratch,
and probably as a profile silhouette. Don't draw too big.
Remember, on the finished map animals are going to reduce to
the size of peppercorns, or peas if you're lucky. Reduce
everything to simple geometric shapes and straight lines. Subtle
changes in the shape of a leg will disappear when the symbol is a
tiny black thing on the map. Go for the essence, and use the
animal's natural attributes: birds fly, so draw them flying; cows
graze, so draw them with their heads down; monkeys swing from
trees, so draw their arms outstretched. These characteristic
natural poses will go a long way to making your symbols show
the essence of what they represent, and their shapes will help
differentiate between the symbols, given that they must appear at
such a minute size.

The map itself contains numerous hand-lettered labels including: ROAD TRIP, GHOST TOWNS, OBLONG, BOGOTA, EFFINGHAM, 45, BIRDS, BIBLE GROVE, MAPLE GROVE, BONE GAP, CRISP, LOUISVILLE, BURNT PRAIRIE, CARBONDALE, MARION TRUCK PLAZA, STOP, FOOD, PATTON'S TRUCK STOP, SHAWNEE TOWN, DEVIL DOGS, HARRIS BURG, 13, EQUALITY, JUNCTION, OLD SHAWNEE TOWN, 57, HODGES PARK, UNITY, THEBES, 3, MOUNDS, KARNAK, JOPPA, FUTURE CITY, CAIRO, MISSISSIPPI RIVER, OHIO RIVER

JONATHON ROSEN

Jonathon Rosen drew this map for Wigwag magazine's "Road Trip" feature. By using symbolic drawings, almost to the exclusion of anything else, Rosen's map shows how few cartographic conventions are needed in this kind of mapmaking. You travel from one symbol to another.

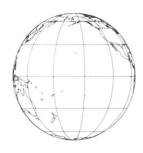

With the help of a computer, the world turns. Once the coordinates are programmed, you can look at earth from any angle. These views rotate the globe in six stages at 0 degrees latitude, the equator.

Computers

For the book, magazine, or newspaper map artist, the computer has many advantages as well as pitfalls. The professional cartographer has long relied on computing to help draw a picture of the bottom of the sea, the bumpy surfaces of the earth, or the shapes of the continents. Once programmed properly, the computer can show you not only a view of any part of the world from any altitude but also from any angle; just command that you need to be four miles above the Suez Canal looking northeast toward the Black Sea, and behold, the genie-map flows out of the magic machine—and all with unassailable accuracy and speed. No more wearisome hand-transference of the little squares on a straight grid to the angled perspective of a bird's eye view projection.

But remember those clichés about the computer: it's a dumb machine; it's only as good as the person using it; garbage in, garbage out (GIGO). GIGO (don't you love computerese?) is important. You can buy programs for desktop publishing that promise to make you a cartographer—just as you can buy chart programs that will make you a statistics expert and word-processing programs that will make you a famous author. Beware.

First, map boundaries do change. At the start of the Persian Gulf War, many maps of the area showed a diamond-shaped neutral zone on the Iraq-Saudi Arabia frontier near Kuwait. That border was ratified two years earlier, but most atlases work in a slower publication cycle than that and were not updated yet. It was suggested by several readers who had seen the diamond shape printed in other magazines and newspapers that *Time* magazine had mistakenly left it off its war maps. So make sure your program is based on the latest available information, and then be prepared to update.

Second, look at how the makers of the computer program have simplified the shorelines. Check them against an atlas you trust. Check an area that you personally know well. Then decide: With a little effort on your part, could you do as well as the program does by starting from scratch with your own version of the areas you need? It will take you longer, but you'll end up with just what you want, and it will be your own work. After all, there is no mystery about the way that country shapes and shorelines get into the program in the first place. The makers of any such program have to do what you would do: trace a line from an established authority—a good atlas, or an official source such as the CIA or the Defense Mapping Agency. Clip art has its place for some types of generic illustration or symbols, but seldom is it any good for maps; however, if all you are looking for is the

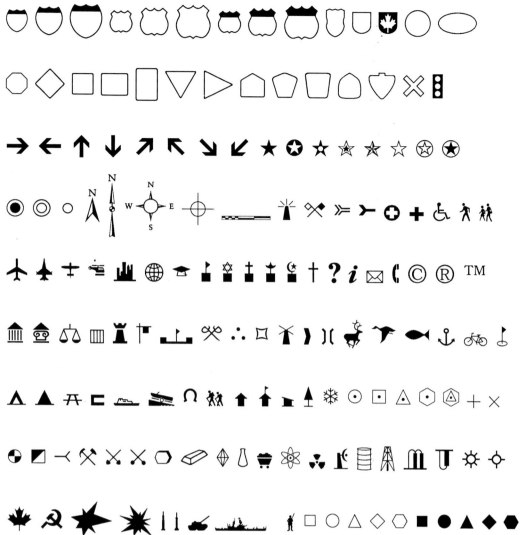

Carta by Adobe Systems is a font of map-symbols for the computer. A selection is shown here. The complete font includes road signs, stars, arrows, scales, compasses, and pictograms and is accessed from the keyboard like a typeface.

backround to a graphic—a wallpaper map-pattern—OK, go to the clip file.

Far more inportant than off-the-shelf computer map programs is the machine itself as a tool for designers. The graphic arts industry has moved almost exclusively toward computer production. This means that if the artists or designers themselves produce digitized images then they will (1) save money on production, because there is no translation of one sort of image (flat art) into a production mode (digital); (2) get a better printed result for the same reason as (1) and because there is no degrading of the image during such a translation into digital information; and (3) be able to produce cleaner, more detailed artwork at a manageable scale, because the artwork does not have to be drawn twice as large as the final print job in order to include all the detail. Good drawing programs, such as Aldus *Freehand* and Adobe *Illustrator,* allow you to see your drawing at eight-times magnification while you are working on it, thus giving you both a degree of accuracy and a view of your work that had

The peaks of population in the United States in 1979, plotted by the Harvard Laboratory for Computer Graphics Mapping Service. Although we know that most people live in the northeast or in the Los Angeles area, it's still a jolt to see what the numbers look like.

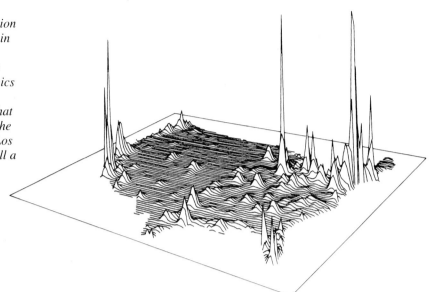

Compressing the travel time between the United States and Europe could be likened to bringing the two continents closer together (above). But faster flying times across the United States itself are hard to show. If you squeeze the map (right), it's no longer a map, it's an illustration.

previously been invisible to the normal human eye. This is especially useful at the end of a long job, when a Damoclean deadline is hanging over you, and production managers are pacing up and down as they wait for the final click of your mouse to pounce on your disk.

The computer's ability to enlarge the image as you work on it is particularly useful in mapmaking, where hundreds of names, dots, symbols, and other geographical details must be attended to. In the days not so long ago when type was cut up into tiny fragments and stuck on the map by hand, some of it inevitably ended up being printed crooked, or it just disappeared into a separator's limbo (probably the floor). Thus, helpful hints about what sort of glue is best for ensuring that parts don't fall off has changed to a much more important discussion about whether those parts say the right thing, contain the right information. The computer has enabled us to take the creation of graphic art to a higher level of finish, while also allowing much more time to ponder the accuracy or appropriateness of the image. And if by chance some part of that image is wrong, or you need to include some new facts, then changing it is a breeze. Once your base maps are in the system, they are easy to find, they don't curl up at the edges, they don't creep to the back of those huge flat filing drawers, but they can be instantly updated.

But back to warnings. The inevitability of the whole system—quality of image, speed of execution, and below all, the economic bottom line—has sucked everyone connected to graphics into a false belief that mapmaking, and all graphic design, is somehow *easier* now that the Mac* is here.

---

*Most of the initial production of graphic art in publishing is currently executed on the various models of Apple's Macintosh. This is not to say map programs will not run on PCs, but that the graphic arts side of the business (as opposed to the *writing*, for instance) has pretty well come down in favor of the Mac.

What you can do to maps (or anything) on a computer is both wonderful and awful. I've discussed the distortions inherent in different noncomputer-generated world projections. Imagine the graphic horrors possible by further distorting them through compression, skewing, or other manipulation of the computer file. It's all too easy. If the map does not fit into the required space indicated on a layout, just squeeze it. The map is too short? Lengthen it. In the service of illustration this may be acceptable, but image manipulation should be used very carefully with maps, because maps are diagrams of information, and you shouldn't mess about with it just because a new shape *looks* nice or fits the space better.

Let's look at two examples. The time it takes to travel across the Atlantic has dropped from months to hours in the five hundred years between sailing in Columbus's nineties and supersonic flying in our nineties. The ability to compress the space of the Atlantic produces a startling effect and makes a good graphic point. It works because there's really nothing to compress (with apologies to marine life). But if you apply the same idea to the shrinking of travel time across the continental United States, all you could do to show it would be to bring the two coasts closer together—easy enough to do with your magic machine. The trouble is that what's left has now ceased to be a map. It's an *illustration*, and an effective one at that. Of course, it could just as well be an illustration for the slimming craze in America or of belt-tightening in an economic recession.

These examples each show a perfectly legitimate use of the computer with very different results. My point is that you must be aware of what you are doing and not imagine that the computer will solve all your mapmaking problems. The computer is a tool without a mind of its own. You have to think for it, then make clear judgments about the output. Know why you have used a particular distortion. Imagine laboriously elongating or compressing the shapes yourself by hand, without the help of a computer. Think about the rationale for changing the shape of a map, and don't just get the machine to change the shape for no better reason than that it is capable of doing so quickly and easily. Anything drawn on a computer must be done on purpose and must not be the result of chance.

Thirteenth-century route maps for travelers depicted roads as straight lines running vertically on a narrow scroll. The road was interrupted by profile drawings of cities and towns that could be recognized by the coachman and passengers as they came into view. These scrolls are the forerunners of automobile computer maps. Bosch-Blaupunkt's Travel Pilot navigation system encodes maps onto compact discs and shows them on a 5-inch

Bosch-Blaupunkt's Travel Pilot is a computer guidance program for the dashboard of your car. The maps are encoded on CDs (five or six cover the U.S.) and displayed on a five-inch screen. Wheel sensors monitor the car's movements.

The Pioneer navigation system uses a network of satellites to provide tracking information for in-car computer maps.

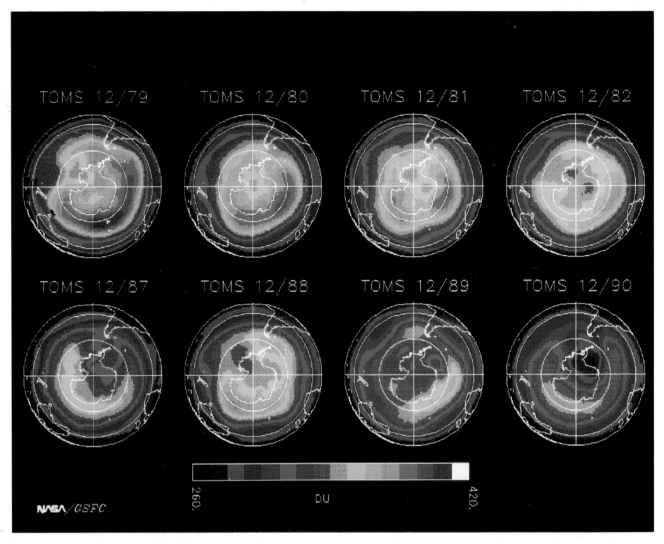

These NASA pictures (for the month of
December, from 1979 to 1990) show how the
ozone hole over Antarctica is getting bigger.
The colors change from warm yellows and reds
in 1979 (high ozone values), to dark blues, and
then to purple and black (less ozone) for the
December 1990 image (detail, right).

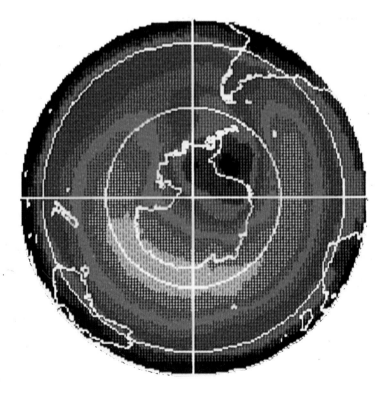

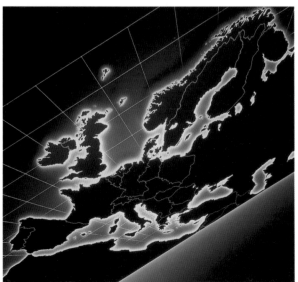

The shapes of the continents here are squeezed, tilted, and combined with a photograph. There is no cartographic value in these images, but they make good science-fiction illustrations.

Vietnam superimposed on the outline of Britain. This is literally bringing a point home—in this case, to British readers—during the Vietnam war. The best way to understand something you don't know is to put it into the context of something you do know.

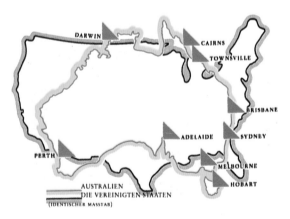

America and Australia have more in common than a language, as you can see when they are brought this close together.

screen on your car's dashboard. Sensors on the vehicle's wheels and an electronic compass keep track of your position and display it on the screen so you can see where you are supposed to be going and also where you actually are. A more sophisticated version of this in-car mapping, with a color screen, has been developed by Pioneer Electric Corporation. It uses satellites instead of wheel sensors to determine where you are. This network of eyes in the sky is the global positioning system currently used by the Department of Defense, and by most aircraft and ships. On the ground, it is accurate to within two car lengths, so if you are late, you'll have to think up a better excuse than getting lost on the way.

We have come to accept computer-enhanced color as a standard for viewing otherwise invisible scientific phenomena. An example of this is the hole in the ozone layer over the Antarctic. The sequence of images of that area shows the emergence in the early eighties, and the subsequent growth, of the "hole" in the protective layer of ozone in the stratosphere. Our use of chlorofluorocarbons (most commonly produced by refrigerators and aerosols) has thinnned this shield from the sun's harmful ultraviolet radiation by as much as 50 percent in the area over the South Pole. Perhaps these maps will convince industry of the urgent necessity to find and use nonpolluting alternatives.

Mapmakers with computers can produce incredible images of the earth. By combining sea-depth measurements with digital information about land elevation, and matching all of that with Landsat satellite images, pictures can be made that are beautiful to look at and perfectly accurate in their detail. For the first time we can draw truly cartographic, pictorial maps. The colors on such maps are still the personal taste of the artist/programmer, and this tends to make them more abstract than real (urban areas, for instance, are shown in tones of red, to better distinguish them from surrounding countryside). But there is something about the concentration of detail that coaxes the viewer to understand these images simultaneously as a diagram of a place and a picture of it.

Scale

The understanding of anything is greatly enhanced by seeing it in the context of something familiar. An orange is gigantic compared to a pinhole, large compared to a walnut, small compared to a basketball, tiny compared to a building, practically nothing compared to the earth. It's the same with statistics. You may know that Aramco, the Saudi Arabian company, produces more oil than anyone else in the world. You may even know what their production is (5.34 million barrels every day). But how much bigger is that than the next largest oil-producing company?

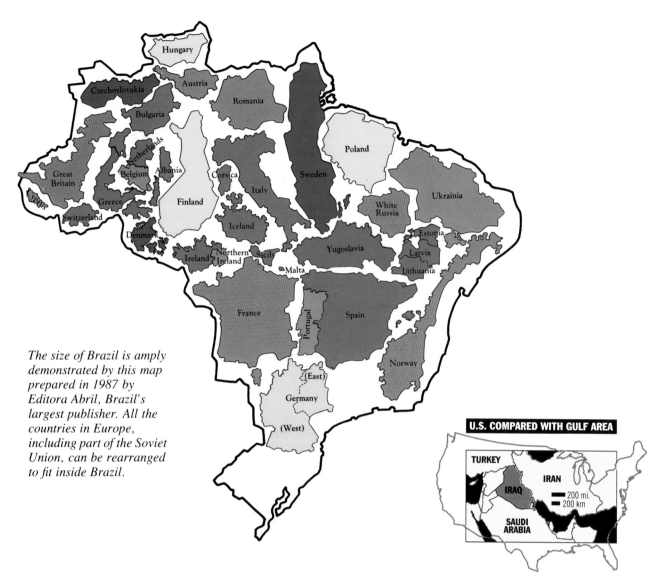

The size of Brazil is amply demonstrated by this map prepared in 1987 by Editora Abril, Brazil's largest publisher. All the countries in Europe, including part of the Soviet Union, can be rearranged to fit inside Brazil.

100,000 barrels? twice as much? (Pemex of Mexico is number two, with a daily production of 2.89 million barrels). And, more important, and closer to home, what are those amounts of oil compared to their reserves? (based on current output, Aramco has a 132 year supply of oil left in the ground before they run out, and Pemex has 49). The context of the additional information helps you understand the original unanchored statistic. In fact, I would go so far as to say that *without* a context, knowing that Aramco produces over 5 million barrels of oil a day is almost meaningless. It only begins to mean something when compared to some aspect of your life: If we continue to rely on imported oil, for example, how long will it last? It puts international quarrels or cooperation in a new light.

Context is important in maps. I lived in England during the Vietnam War, and nothing brought the war home to me better than a map of Vietnam drawn at the same scale and superimposed on a map of England. I instantly understood the distances involved, because I could relate them to distances I knew.

During the Persian Gulf War this map helped Time's readers understand the size of the war zone. Kuwait is shown to be about the size of Connecticut.

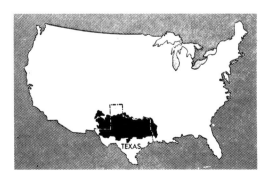

This is from an encyclopedia published in the 1930s. Turkey, with an area of 296,110 square miles, is slightly larger than Texas, which has an area of 267,340 square miles.

Of course maps must always have a scale rule on them. More and more clients want to internationalize themselves, or at least not appear too insular, and will ask for the scale to be in miles and kilometers. It is a good idea to relate that scale to something that a reader can identify with. Relate the size of the Middle East to that of the United States. Show how big Brazil is by fitting a number of smaller countries inside its borders. Move countries out of their normal atlas or globe context, and give them a new neighbor. Richard Saul Wurman has done this with urban areas. He got a group of his students to make same-scale (600 feet-to-an-inch) models of fifty significant towns and cities, old and new, from ancient Babylon to Moscow, ancient Athens to Washington, D.C. His premise was that you think of these places in a vacuum, but have no idea of how they relate to each other in size or to a city that you know.

Mercator's map had distortions of scale on it, because it was drawn as a course-plotting navigational aid for the mariners of the sixteenth century. His map became the standard schoolroom projection, and as a result, we are left with wrong ideas about the size relationships of many countries. You can help correct these misconceptions by showing countries in the correct scale to one another when you have the appropriate opportunity.

Distortion

The cartogram is a device that combines cartography and statistical charting. The idea is to apply a numerical value to a geographic region. An example might show oil-producing nations drawn in proportion to the amount of oil they produce. That could be compared to coal-producers, drawn in *their* relationships. Countries that produce more oil or coal grow in relation to their true geographic size, others get smaller. The success of this kind of diagrammatic mapping depends on readers knowing their geography, at least to the extent of recognizing that it has been tampered with for the sake of statistical comparison. It is a very potent graphic tool but it is underused because editors and clients suspect a general lack of geographic knowledge on the part of their readers, and distortion of this type could cloud the message on the map rather than illuminate it. You can judge from the examples here whether or not it is a worthwhile thing to do. If you agree that it *is* a viable way to show information, be careful when plotting such graphics. It is important to stick to mathematical principles in working out the size of each area. Never change a shape by measuring the maximum north-south distance and enlarging the whole thing by a percentage that represents its relative size to the whole. Not only will you be increasing the height but the width as well, resulting in a whole

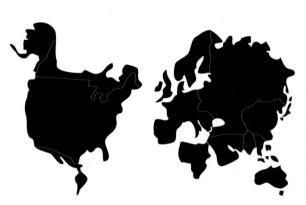

The world of coal (above), and oil (below), from a study by Exxon. Countries are redrawn proportionate to their reserves of energy sources. More than half of the world's oil is in the Middle East—it couldn't be clearer.

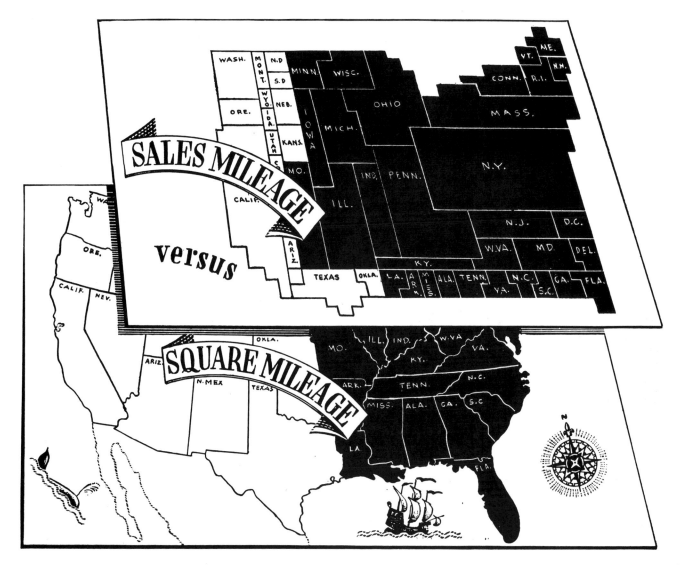

America as it looks when the states are drawn in proportion to business transacted. The Mutual Broadcasting System (of advertising) used comparative maps in the 1940s to show people the value of sales mileage over geographical mileage.

different kind of distortion. To do it properly, you must divide all areas of the map into equal units, probably little squares, then increase or decrease the number of units—but not their size—for each geographical area according to the new proportions you want to show. You should end up with the same number of squares in both your new map and the original. You have simply arranged them differently. Keeping the look of the original, that recognizable geographic shape that you want to echo, is a matter of trial and error. You will be constantly reshuffling the given number of pieces until you arrive at a satisfactory final shape. The smaller the original units, the more easily you can approximate the look of the countries' borders. If you choose a relatively large original unit, the end result will have the stair-stepped appearance of a pixeled computer image—which may not necessarily be a bad thing: it can help alert the reader to the fact that this is a diagram, not cartography.

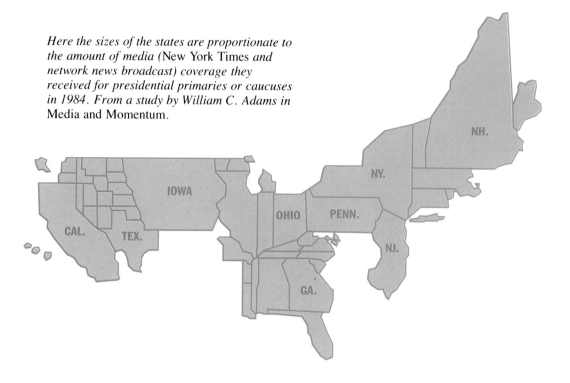

Here the sizes of the states are proportionate to the amount of media (New York Times and network news broadcast) coverage they received for presidential primaries or caucuses in 1984. From a study by William C. Adams in Media and Momentum.

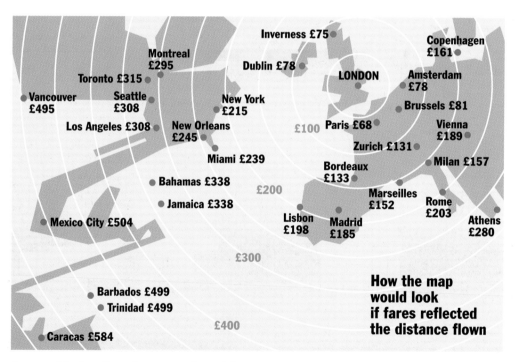

A map with shorelines drawn to reflect airfares from London, rather than mileage. Europe, where state-owned airlines charge up to five times as much as U.S. airlines, is enlarged. North America has shrunk proportionately, and Los Angeles is approximately the same distance from London as Athens (L.A. is actually four times further away).

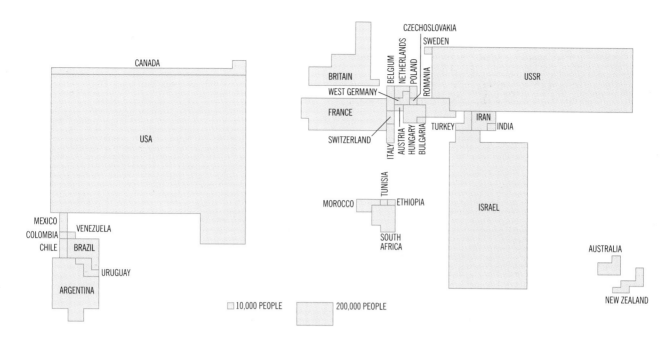

The distribution of the world's Jewish population in 1987.

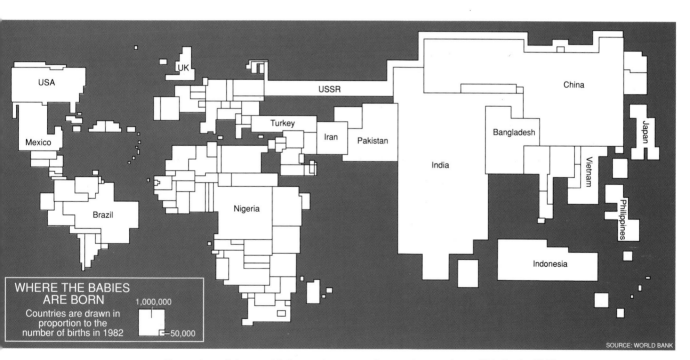

Countries of the world drawn in proportion to the number of births in 1982.

7

The Fun Part

**Metaphorical maps
Maps for friends
Other "friendly maps"
Jokes**

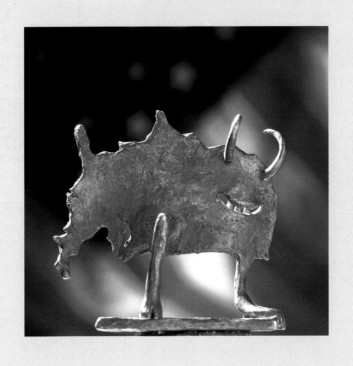

The fun part: why just this chapter? I think *all* mapmaking should be fun. Maybe you've gathered this from earlier parts of the book. But some maps are actually intended to be funny, while others, with serious intentions, are merely fun to make. In this chapter is a collection of maps that transform the geographical boundaries of countries into nongeographic objects or even people. Next, there's a section on drawing maps to give directions to your friends, followed by some examples of relaxed hand-drawn location maps. Last, and probably least, are real joke maps.

Metaphorical Maps

Visual jokes are often based on an image that appears to the eye first as one thing, then a second later as something else. Maps can go through this metamorphosis without changing their shape (''maptical'' illusions). The first impression of what you see is always a *map*. On closer inspection a map might become a collection of Europeans, a dog's head, or an ex-prime minister of Britain. You could probably think up other images to fit into the shape of a shoreline, but unless what you thought of was appropriate to the subject, it would be perversely pointless. The only reason for transforming a map in this way is to add meaning to the cartography: here's a map, and here also is a picture to help you understand what the map's about. Not the *geography*, the *ideology*.

It's an old art. The earliest example here dates from 1617 and can easily be read as both a map of the Netherlands and the majestic lion that stands for the importance of the Low Countries' commanding location as a center of world trade. Nothing is forced here; the lion works well both as an artistic and a political device, and you can read the information on the map as well as if it were unembellished.

The picture has taken over to a greater extent in the maps of Europe pictured here; and by 1985 David Suter is wreaking such havoc with the countries of the Common Market that their shapes are almost completely subservient to the notion of the struggle between the working class and the upper class within these places. Suter is using the map merely as a starting point to let the reader know that the subject of his illustration is Europe: He's not interested in giving us a geography lesson, but instead is happy to allude to the shapes of England, the Germanies (there were two then), Spain, and France, as long as they make conveniently grappling arm and leg shapes. In the hands of such an artist these complex map-drawings work, but few can pull it off.

In 1811, Elbridge Gerry, the governor of Massachusetts, changed the map of his state districts to include more of the

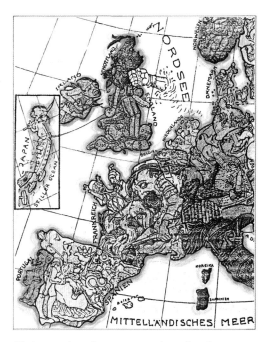

Fitting national stereotypes into the shapes of their home countries is a touchy thing in our enlightened era. But in 1914, when this German artist's view of Europe was drawn (detail), it was war-time, and propaganda knew no restrictions.

Boundaries on maps are changed for three reasons. First, in the early days of cartography, mistakes in copying or newly discovered information made mapmakers readjust their drawings. Second, throughout history, hostile invasions have led the rulers of the victorious countries to claim the stolen territory as their own. Third, politicians redraw maps to suit their own electoral ends. In this third category—redistricting—is Elbridge Gerry's 1811 map of Essex County, Massachusetts. Drawn by Gilbert Stewart to resemble a salamander, this map gave rise to the term gerrymander.

There is a lot going on in this 1870 map of Europe. England is an isolated old woman with Ireland in tow. The roof of the little Swiss chalet is also a shovel that France is using to repel Prussia's advances. Italy is holding Prussia back, too. Russia is angrily poised to fill up the basket on its back. Corsica and Sardinia are giggling at the whole thing.

The map of the seventeen provinces of Netherlands is from Germania Inferior by Petrus Montanus, engraved and published in Amsterdam in 1617. This is a beautiful example of the picture-as-map, as well as the map-as-picture.

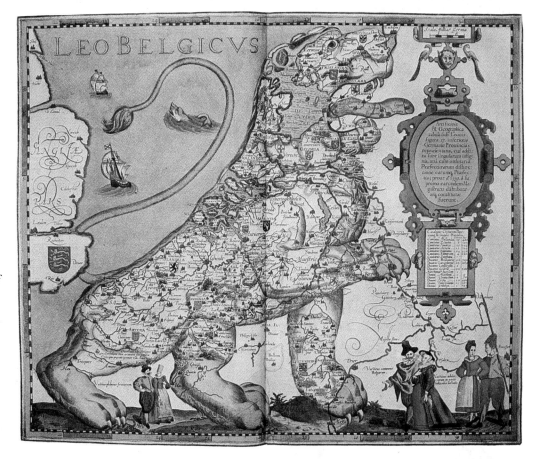

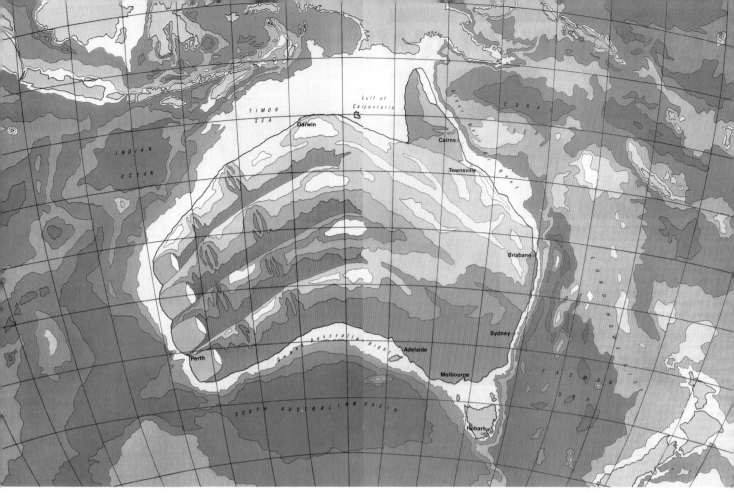

In this advertisement, which ran in Punch, *the 150-year-old British humor weekly, the map of Australia is drawn as the back of a hand. The advertiser's claim to know Australia well is thus achieved with a wit well-suited to* Punch.

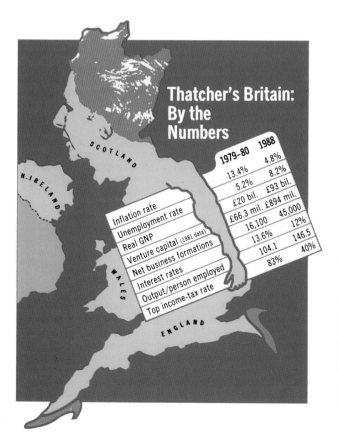

Here are statistics about Thatcher's Britain from a 1988 article in Inc. *magazine. Sometimes the shape of a country can be the shape of something else at the same time—in this case, the prime minister. The western coast of Scotland was transformed to a profile of the Iron Lady.*

David Suter's drawing of the struggle within Europe recalls an earlier era (around 1850) when it was more common to manipulate map images. This ran in Time *magazine in 1989 on the eve of a European summit in Madrid that looked as though it would be full of internal squabbling.*

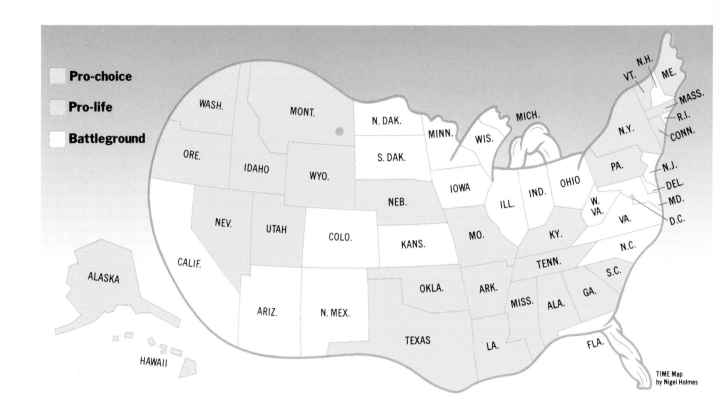

Pro-choice

Pro-life

Battleground

WASH.
MONT.
N. DAK.
MINN.
MICH.
VT. N.H.
ME.
MASS.
R.I.
CONN.
ORE.
IDAHO
WYO.
S. DAK.
WIS.
N.Y.
PA.
ALASKA
NEV.
UTAH
COLO.
NEB.
IOWA
ILL.
IND.
OHIO
W. VA.
VA.
N.J.
DEL.
MD.
D.C.
CALIF.
KANS.
MO.
KY.
N.C.
ARIZ.
N. MEX.
OKLA.
ARK.
TENN.
S.C.
HAWAII
TEXAS
LA.
MISS.
ALA.
GA.
FLA.

TIME Map
by Nigel Holmes

The abortion map that never ran: Pressure from researchers within Time led to this image being withdrawn an hour before the press deadline. In its place, Time used an unillustrated map—itself a testament to the speed with which computers can get things together. We all learned a lesson about the power of pictures. These sketches preceded the abortion map. The similarity between the shape of the U.S. and a fetus suggested the possibility of combining the two. Using a photograph of a 10-week-old fetus as reference, I superimposed it on the map. Florida became the umbilical cord.

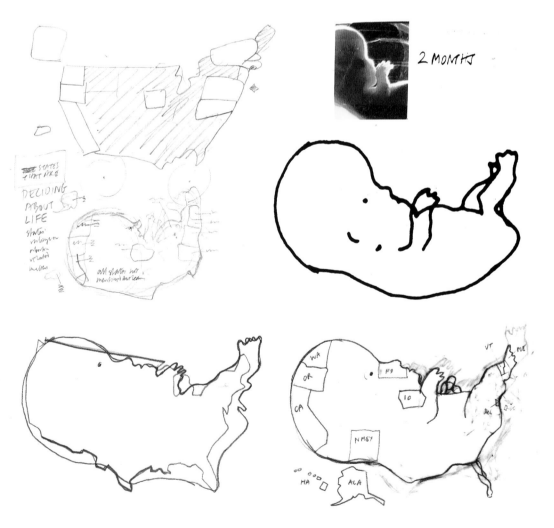

2 MONTHS

electorate likely to vote for two members of his party and to ensure their election to the Senate. The resulting redistricted map of Essex County was drawn by Gilbert Stewart, a political cartoonist of the day, to resemble a salamander, and so was born the *gerrymander,* or division of a state into election districts ''so as to give one political party a majority in many districts while concentrating the voting strength of the other party into as few districts as possible'' *(Random House Dictionary).* Gerry went on to become James Madison's second vice-president, but he died in office in 1814, leaving cartographers a great excuse to find interesting combinations of shape within maps.

During the summer of 1989, the two sides of the abortion question came face-to-face with one another in a series of demonstrations aimed at influencing the Supreme Court's possible decision to reverse the *Roe v. Wade* ruling of 1973, which had established the right to terminate a pregnancy. *Time* magazine needed a map that showed which way state legislatures were leaning on the question: whether to allow abortion (so-called Pro Choice) or not (Pro-Life). Those definitions always bothered me. They represent opposing views but neither one calls themselves the true verbal opposite of the other. I can certainly understand that ''Pro-Death'' or ''Anti-Choice'' just doesn't sound right to them. Both are touchy definitions, as I found out.

While thinking about how to present the information—three simple categories: Pro-Choice states, Pro-Life states, undecided states (we called them ''battleground'' states)—I noticed the similarity between the shape of a fetus and the shape of the United States. I suggested to *Time's* editor, Henry Muller, that this might be a sensitive paring of images for our readers, although I personally felt that it was a perfect match. The fetus that I drew was ten weeks old. The medical profession does not consider so young a fetus to be a viable human being; in fact, it only becomes that at twenty-five weeks. Nevertheless the very presence on our map of a human-looking blob—for it looks remarkably well formed even at such an early stage of its development—was too much for some of the researchers on *Time's* staff. Eventually they put such a strong case to the editor that he felt we should not run the map in that form.* While agreeing with me about the appropriateness of the image, Henry Muller judged that if three members of our staff were so upset by it, then enough readers would also be. And if readers were upset with the image, they would overlook the *content,* the *information* on the map, and the point of the graphic would be lost in the heat

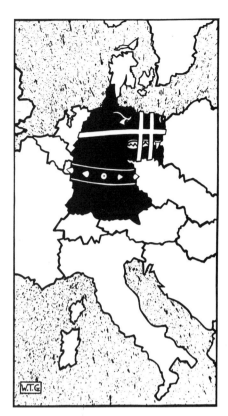

Bill Gibbons drew this political cartoon of the two Germanies in the shape of a vicious muzzled dog. The fear that a soon-to-be-reunified country might once again be a force for evil spawned many such images during 1990.

Peter Brookes's brilliant combination of Italy, Sicily, and the Mafia, published in the London Times *in 1986.*

---

*Their argument was that it was hard to judge the age of the fetus from the drawing, and that just by being there, it seemed to have a Pro-Life bias. They were right: Even I was amazed at just how life-like a medically *unviable* fetus looks, and it no doubt came as a bit of a shock to my correctly cautious colleagues also that it should look so completely human.

Holling Clancy wrote and illustrated children's books in the 1940s and 1950s that are part good old-fashioned adventure story, fantasy illustration, and natural history textbook. Wide margins contain carefully researched drawings on the geography and past history of the places visited by the book's characters. These books can be looked at by young nonreaders, read as stories by seven-year-olds, or studied by an older age group.

In the map transformations shown here, from Paddle-to-the-Sea, *Clancy notices the similarities between the shapes of shorelines and living things.*

of their indignation. So we ran a simple map of the states. The lesson here is that even though an image may be right, it could be too powerful for some delicate situations.

Maps for Friends

"How do I find your place?" Those of us who have lived in out-of-the-way places, or have friends who do, have faced this question. It gets worse when the other party says: "I'll draw you a map—I have this great back way that will keep you away from the traffic/crowds/town/fish-packing factory smells." If only all roads had signs just where you need them. They don't, of course, most especially in your friends' out-of-the-way places.

It would be a miracle if you lived where the sun was always clearly in view on the horizon, and you could instruct your early evening guests to simply drive toward the sun on a particular road, until they saw the brick house at the end. It is much more likely that you live where it's occasionally cloudy, you can't see a horizon, all the houses are brick, more than one road approaches it, and guests might arrive at any time of day or night.

Very few of us are truly oriented so that we know which way we are going, but something to remember about driving or walking or cycling is that when you are actually *on* the road, it appears in front of you in a straight line.

Early coaching maps capitalized on this perception. What these route plans noted very accurately was not the direction of the road, but the distances between easily identified landmarks along the way, and on which side of the road they would be seen. John Ogilby, a seventeenth-century English mapmaker and surveyor, measured the distance between London and Berwick (on the Scottish border) and drew the route as one straight line using an ingenious scroll-like device. This was the first time statute miles* were used for such calculations, and the official distances for this journey changed from 260 to 340 miles. Since there was no way of recording the passing miles on the journey, passengers were used to calculating the length of their trip in days and hours. A known distance of 260 miles would have taken far less time then than the 360 miles that this journey had now become. There must have been quite a bit of confusion until statute miles became the norm. Ogilby's maps were published in a 100-map road atlas after his death in 1676. Just so that travelers knew the general direction in which they were headed, a compass oriented northward was included on each stretch of the scroll.

I remember a service that the British Automobile Association made available to its members. It was a direct descendant of

---

*The English statute mile is equal to 5,280 feet.

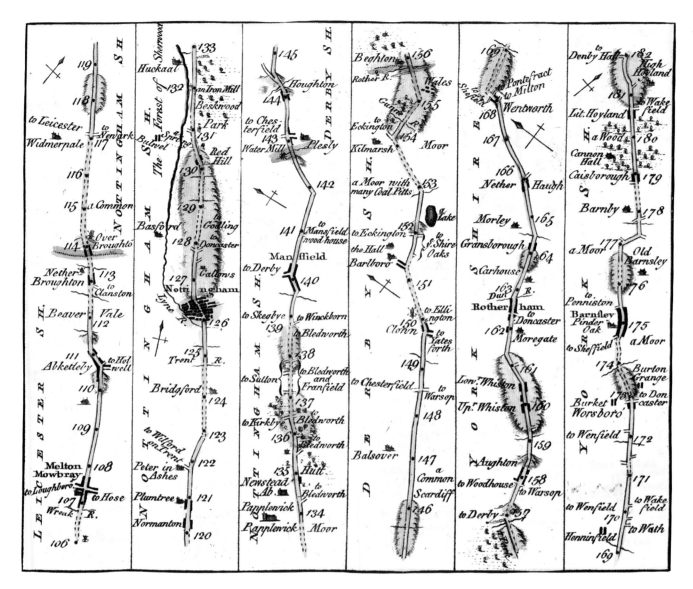

Ogilby's maps, and it got you from one point in England to another via the shortest route. The map they provided was a straight line going up the middle of a four-by-nine-inch strip of paper, and it noted what you'd be passing, what roads crossed your path, and what the mileage was between all these points. On the cover it would say: ''Nottingham to Cambridge, 134 Miles.''

Maps for friends can be as simple as that. The most direct way to make sure someone finds you is to note the distances between landmarks you'll see on the way. Before making the map, do the trip yourself: Try to experience it through the eyes of someone who has never been along these roads that are so familiar to you that you may not even know their names. What *exactly* do you see on the way, and how far *is* it from that bar in the town to the barn on the road home where you turn left? It can be quite revealing to yourself to note it all down, and although the end result may not look like a map—more like a list of places passed—it's the most reliable directional help you could give.

Coaching maps operated on a simple premise: When you are in the coach, the road stretches out in a straight line before you. Thus a map could be shown as a basically straight line, showing towns and landmarks passed en route. This is a map of a section of rural England from 1782.

179

To find a private boarding school without getting lost in the countryside of Southern England, a number of easily missed road junctions are emphasized in this map more clearly than on ''official'' maps of the area. The elimination of alternative roads is one way that hand-drawn maps for friends can help in finding a specific destination.

HOW TO FIND BROCKHURST SCHOOL

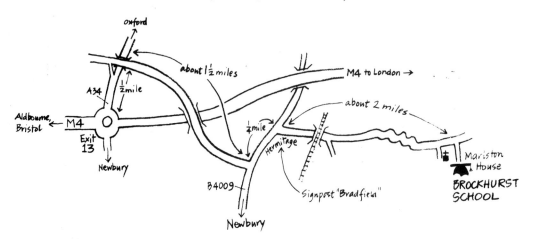

This relaxed hand-drawn map from an advertisement for Einstein Moomjy, the carpet company, might help to put customers in a relaxed mood; a good way to reduce the tension of home-furnishing decisions.

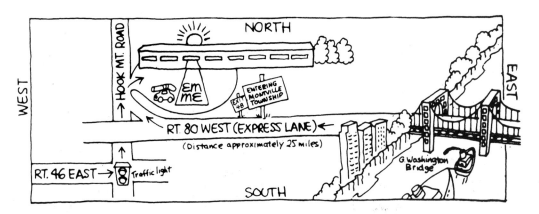

Robert Lockwood sent me this map when I visited him from New York. He is an expert on communication and information graphics, so it was natural for him to give me visual help. As a tool, it worked perfectly. (But if you want to visit him, beware. He's moved to Maine.)

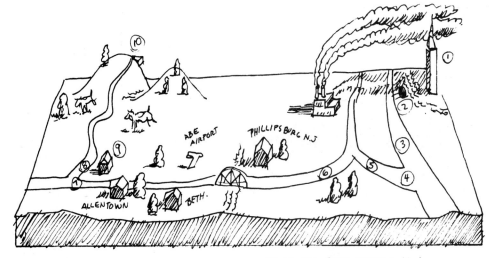

1. NEW YORK CITY
2. LINCOLN TUNNEL
3. N.J. TURNPIKE
4. EXIT 10
5. Rt. 287

6. Rt. 78 TO CLINTON AND PHILLIPSBURG N.J.
7. TREXLERTOWN, FOLGELSVILLE EXIT
8. Rt. 100 NORTH
9. SHANKWEILLERS REST. CALL 298-2295 FOR DETAILS TO 10
10. RECOMPENSE

Other "Friendly" Maps

Artists are fond of making maps of where they live, and a couple of examples are reproduced here. To gain attention, commercial maps are sometimes deliberately drawn as though they are just throwaway, casual things that visually imply that they will give you some general direction without being too serious about it. Their relaxed nature reflects the subject matter and makes it more accessible, whether it's about the shops on Rodeo Drive or shows the way around the campus of the Rhode Island School of Design. If, however, you are about to drop $1,000 for a leather belt, or are just starting as a student in a strange place, you may not be all that relaxed, thus the informality of the maps might help. There is something about the evidence of the human touch, the slightly wavering line, the not-so-straight lettering, the little mistake, that endears the reader. It makes the reader feel at home in a place that may otherwise be difficult to understand. Humanized maps can help when geography gets in the way.

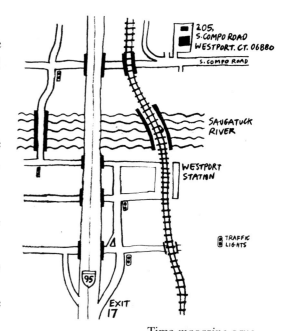

Time *magazine gave this map to a courier company that brings proofs to my home for checking. One day a driver said to me, ''These are great directions, I found your place easily. Who did this map?'' When I told him that I had drawn it, he replied, ''It's very professional. You should do this sort of thing for a living.''*

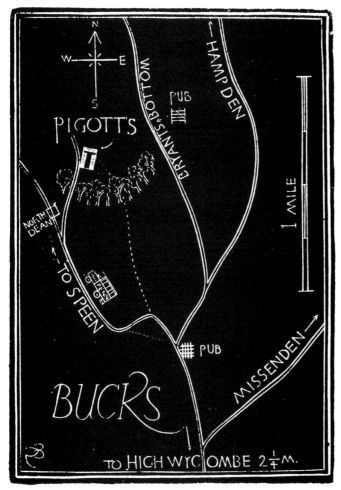

A classically simple white-line wood engraving of the directions to his home made by Eric Gill in 1928. How elegant just a few lines can be. Fun, too: see the pubs?

A flyer for Harbor Sweets, a candy store in Salem, Massachusetts. This playful little map recalls childhood memories of simpler times.

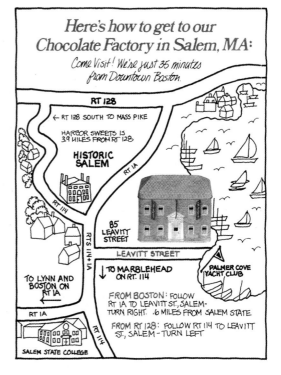

Welcome

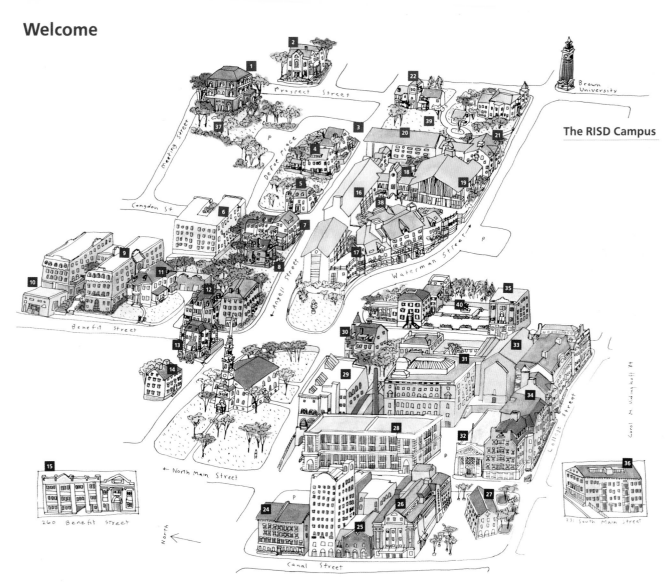

The RISD Campus

Finding your way around a new campus is a daunting experience. This friendly treatment of the Rhode Island School of Design's hilly campus goes a long way to help nervous newcomers feel at home. Carol Vidinghoff's charming drawings of the buildings are both accurate and inviting.

The names of the high-priced clothing stores are the most important features on a map of Rodeo Drive, Los Angeles. The street itself can be graphically reduced to a single, throwaway squiggle.

BRIGHTON WAY

GUCCI		CARTIER
HERMÈS		UPSTAIRS GALLERY
DYANSEN GALLERY OF BEVERLY HILLS		ANDREA CARRANO
TOMMY HILFIGER		BERNINI
BARDELLI		BEVERLY RODEO HOTEL
CHÂTELAINE	**R**	CAFE RODEO
TED LAPIDUS	**O**	BASSINI
GIORGIO BEVERLY HILLS	**D**	BENETTON/012 BENETTON
HANSON GALLERY	**E**	CHRISTIE'S
ADRIENNE VITTADINI	**O**	AMIR MOZAFARIAN
UNGARO		ZIMMELMAN & SONS
NATIONAL HERITAGE GALLERY OF FINE ART	**D**	BALLY OF SWITZERLAND/MEN'S
ALAÏA CHEZ GALLAY	**R**	VILLEROY & BOCH
HAMMACHER SCHLEMMER	**I**	ATTINA
LOUIS VUITTON	**V**	DIAMONDS ON RODEO
SIMIC GALLERY	**E**	LAISE ADZER
CHANEL BOUTIQUE		ROMERO SALON

ATTINA
DIAMONDS ON RODEO
LAISE ADZER
ROMERO SALON
DAVID ORGELL
BOWLES-SOROKKO GALLERIES
GEORGETTE KLINGER
FRANCES KLEIN ANTIQUE & ESTATE JEWELS
SOTHEBY'S
BATTAGLIA
VAN CLEEF & ARPELS

DAYTON WAY

FRED HAYMAN BEVERLY HILLS	TWO RODEO (OPENING 1990)
DENMARK JEWELERS	
ALFRED DUNHILL OF LONDON	
MONTRER	

Jokes: A Laughing Matter

I suppose everything gets lampooned sooner or later. Certainly maps are a target for fun. Maybe they are thought of as inherently serious, therefore an easy target. The more seriously something takes itself, the more easily it can be knocked off its pedestal. Just as we have seen how taking liberties with a projection, a shoreline, or a continental shape can result in a striking new vision of a country, so cartoonists with no geographical intent have put familiar country shapes in odd contexts to make us laugh. Some graphically join two ideas, one geographic and one animal: the British cow, for instance. Some are good, punning fantasy: Wrong Island, for example, or the map of Iraq, drawn at a time when the world waited to see what the protagonists would do next in the Persian Gulf. Funniest of all is Pushpin's *Coitus Topographicus,* a drawing of a couple in action with anatomical details wittily drawn and labeled to look like features on a real map.

It is important to keep a sense of humor in all things. To have written a book about maps without some nonsensical fun in it would seem to me to be very wrong. I think the best commercial art is produced when people are having a good time, even though they may be dead serious about what they are doing. Do you understand what I am saying? Or do I have to draw you a map?

A cow's black-and-white markings offer great graphic possibilities. A map of Britain is a particularly appropriate alternative to nature's random splotches of black on this British Holstein (from a wood engraving).

Gary Hallgren's ''Wrong Island'' Christmas card is filled with terrible puns on the names of the real Long Island towns. Like McGehee's astronomical jokes, Hallgren's is a clever pastiche of the ''welcome to'' genre of picture postcard.

An example from a 1986 series of very funny astronomical postcards by Paul McGehee. The joke here is that maps of the universe are made to appear as natural as map-cards of anywhere on earth. The sort of card you'd send to friends saying "wish you were here."

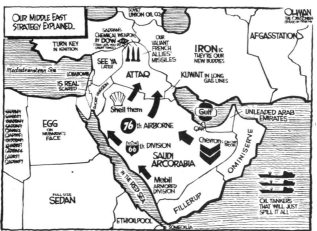

A political cartoon from the early days of the Persian Gulf War. Regularly published use of humor during war-time goes back to Punch's coverage of World War I. Even when soldiers are dying it is possible to draw funny cartoons without offending.

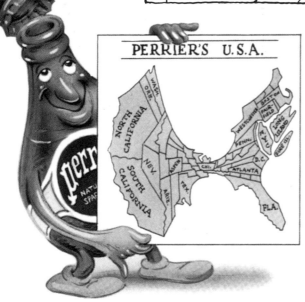

This drawing by Steve Bliss (from Punch, *1990) takes an irreverent look at the way various countries make jokes about one another.*

Robert Grossman's airbrush drawings have enlivened the pages of magazines around the world since the early sixties. Here in two drawings from an Adweek *supplement on American market areas, published in 1980, Grossman turns his caricaturing skills to two icons of the eighties. He turns Vanderbilt jeans and Perrier into maps of their respective strong points.*

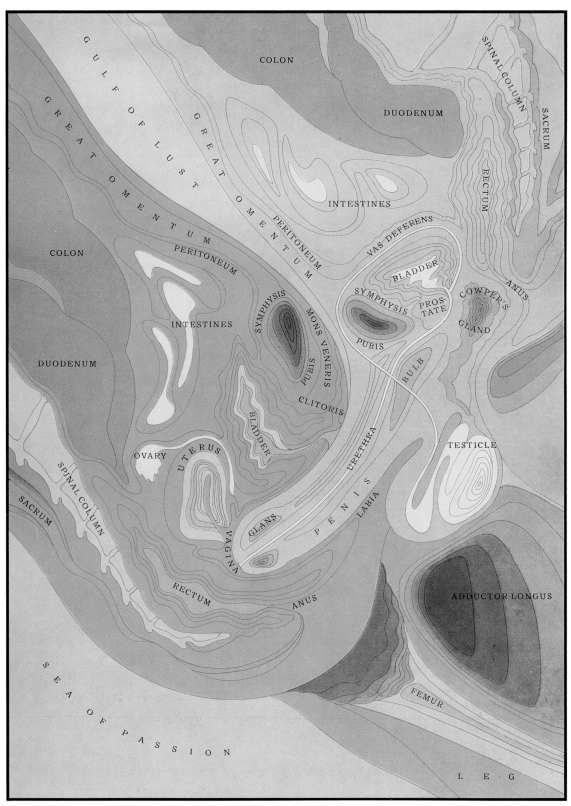

A map of lovemaking by Seymour Chwast from the ''Couples'' edition (March 1980) of Push Pin Graphic. *The clinical, deadpan, cartographic approach to this delicate subject is achieved with consummate subtlety and wit. The colors of the original add to the double take; they parody the pastel shades of a commercial atlas.*

WHERE TO FIND MAPS

Individual Maps

CIA,
Public Affairs Office, Washington, D.C. 20505
Catalog available

Defense Mapping Agency,
Office of Distribution Services, Washington, D.C. 20315
Catalog available

Hubbard,
PO Box 104, Northbrook, Illinois 60065
Three-dimensional plastic maps, mail order

National Geographic Society,
17th & M Streets NW, Washington, D.C. 20036
Subscribe to the magazine and you'll get the best-looking maps currently produced. You can also visit the Society's headquarters, where they sell other maps and related material.

Raven Maps and Images,
34 North Central Avenue, Medford, Oregon 97501
Detailed shaded relief maps developed from the U.S. Geological Survey of selected Western states, Alaska, and Hawaii available; also digital views of land-forms and ocean floors.

U.S. Geological Survey,
Maps Division, Building 41, Federal Center,
Box 25286, Denver, Colorado 80225

Stores

The Map Store Inc.,
1636 Eye Street NW, Washington, D.C. 20006
Map projections, atlases, solid and inflatable globes, and all manner of objects decorated with maps (shower curtains, umbrellas, etc.). Mail order catalog.

Rand McNally,
P.O. Box 7600, Chicago, Illinois 60680
The largest private map producer in the U.S. stocks atlases and map-related material of all types. Stores in New York, Chicago and San Francisco.

Old Maps

Argosy Bookstore,
116 East 59th Street, New York, New York 10022
Upstairs, in the back, is a well-organized selection of antique maps covering all areas of the world. For colored maps, ask whether they are originals: some of the more popular maps are reprints that have been colored by the staff.

Richard B. Arkway Inc.,
538 Madison Avenue, New York, New York 10022

Historic Urban Plans,
Box 276, Ithaca, New York 14851
A great collection of moderately priced facsimiles of city maps from around the world, starting in the sixteenth century.

The Old Print Gallery,
1220 31st Street NW, Washington, D.C. 20007

Philadelphia Print Shop Ltd.,
8441 Germantown Avenue,
Philadelphia, Pennsylvania 19118

G. Robinson,
124 D Bent Street, Taos, New Mexico 87571

BIBLIOGRAPHY

History

Brown, Lloyd A. *Map Making*. Boston: Little, Brown & Co., 1960.

Bricker, Charles, and R. V. Tooley. *Landmarks of Mapmaking*. Brussels: Elsevier-Sequoia, 1968.

Daly, Charles P. "Early History of Cartography." *Journal of the American Geographical Society* 11 (1879).

Generosus, W. S., trans. *Historia Mundi* (Mercator's *Atlas*). London: Michael Sparke, 1635.

George, Wilma. *Animals and Maps*. Berkeley and Los Angeles: University of California Press, 1969.

Harley, J. B., and David Woodward, eds. *The History of Cartography*. Vol. 1. Chicago: University of Chicago Press, 1987.

Hogben, Lancelot. *From Cave Painting to Comic Strip*. New York: Chanticleer Press, 1949.

Howse, Derek, and Michael Sanderson. *The Sea Chart*. New York: McGraw-Hill, 1973.

Lynam, Edward. *The First Engraved Atlas of the World* (Ptolemy's *Cosmographia*). Jenkintown, Pa.: George H. Bean's Library, 1941.

Noble, John Wilford. *The Map Makers*. New York: Alfred A. Knopf, 1981.

Raisz, Erwin. *General Cartography*. New York: McGraw-Hill, 1948.

———. *Mapping the World*. New York: Abelard Schuman Ltd., 1956.

Robinson, Arthur H. *Elements of Cartography*. New York: John Wiley & Sons Inc., 1953.

Skelton, R. A. *Decorative Printed Maps of the Fifteenth to Eighteenth Centuries*. London: Spring Books, 1952.

Speed, John. *Prospect of the Most Famous Parts of the World*. London: William Humble, 1646.

———. *Theatre of the Empire of Great Britaine*. London: George Humble, 1627.

Stevenson, Edward L., trans. *Geography of Claudius Ptolemy*. New York: New York Public Library, 1932.

Tooley, R. V. *Maps and Map Makers*. London: B. T. Batsford Ltd., 1949.

Projections and Relief Mapping

American Cartographic Association. *Matching the Map Projection to the Need*. Bethesda, Md.: American Cartographic Association, 1991.

Raisz, Erwin. *General Cartography*. New York: McGraw-Hill, 1948.

Robinson, Arthur H. *Elements of Cartography*. New York: John Wiley & Sons Inc., 1953.

Other

Child, Heather. *Decorative Maps*. London: Studio Publications, 1956.

Harrison, Richard Edes. *Look at the World (The Fortune Atlas for World Strategy)*.

Makower, Joel, ed. *The Map Catalog: Every Kind of Map and Chart on Earth and Even Some above It*. New York: Vintage Books, 1986. Get this, and you won't need another source list.

The Map Collector (48 High Street, Tring, Hertfordshire HP 235BH, England, U.K.). A quarterly magazine for aficionados.

Southworth, Michael and Susan. *Maps*. Boston: Little, Brown & Co., 1982.

Wurman, Richard Saul. *USAtlas*. New York: Atlas Press, 1990. Wurman's new road atlas of the United States is ingenious in that it rejects the convention of alphabetical, state-by-state construction for 250-square-mile blocks.

CREDITS

INDEX